THE CUCKOO CLOCK

See page 44

'*Are you comfortable?*' inquired the cuckoo

THE
CUCKOO CLOCK

by Mrs Molesworth

Illustrated with line drawings
and colour plates by
E. H. SHEPARD

LONDON: J. M. DENT & SONS LTD
NEW YORK: E. P. DUTTON & CO. INC.

MARY LOUISA STEWART (Mrs Molesworth) was born at Rotterdam, Holland, on 29th May 1839, and died in London on 20th July 1921.

From the age of two, Louisa lived in Manchester: at first in the 'dull house in a dull street' which became the home of Geraldine in 'The Carved Lions' (1895) and of Little Miss Peggy in the book named after her, and later in the much pleasanter suburb of Whalley Range. She spent a year at school in Switzerland, but otherwise was taught at home, and had lessons from Mr and Mrs Gaskell.

In 1861 she married Major Richard Molesworth, and lived for some years at Tabley in Cheshire, and then at High Legh, which had become her parents' home. She had three sons and four daughters, but two of them died as small children; and later she went to live in France and Germany, before settling in London.

She began her career as a writer with four novels published under the pen-name of 'Ennis Graham', and was still using it for her first children's books, of which the earliest, 'Tell me a Story', was published in 1875. 'Carrots' (1876) made her famous, and 'The Cuckoo Clock' (1877) is still her most popular book. The 'old house' described in it was the home of Josephine and Thomas Grindal in Ludlow; but she was also thinking of her grandmother's house in Dunfermline, which she visited as a child.

Mrs Molesworth wrote many other books, most of which are still worth reading. Among the best are 'The Tapestry Room' (1879), 'Two Little Waifs' (1883), 'Four Winds Farm' (1886), 'Nurse Heatherdale's Story' (1891), 'The Carved Lions' (1895), 'Peterkin' (1902) and 'Fairies Afield' (1911).

'Any chapter of "The Cuckoo Clock"', wrote Swinburne in 1884, 'is worth a shoal of the very best novels dealing with the characters and fortunes of mere adults.'

All rights reserved. Made in Great Britain at the Aldine Press, Letchworth, Herts, for J. M. Dent & Sons Ltd, Aldine House, Bedford Street, London. First published 1877. First published in this edition 1954. Last reprinted 1967.

TO

MARY JOSEPHINE

AND TO THE DEAR MEMORY OF HER BROTHER

THOMAS GRINDAL

BOTH FRIENDLY LITTLE CRITICS OF

MY CHILDREN'S STORIES

EDINBURGH, 1877

'Now, these little folks. like most girls and boys,
Loved fairy tales even better than toys.

.   .   .   .   .

And they knew that in flowers on the spray
Tiny spirits are hidden away,
That frisk at night on the forest green,
When earth is bathed in dewy sheen—
And shining halls of pearl and gem,
The Regions of Fancy—were open to them.'

'. . . just as any little child has been guided towards the true
paradise by its fairy dreams of bliss.'   E. A. ABBOTT.

CONTENTS

ILLUSTRATIONS

Colour

Black and White

ix

The Old House

Somewhat back from the village street
Stands the old-fashioned country seat.

ONCE upon a time in an old town, in an old street, there
stood a very old house. Such a house as you could
hardly find nowadays, however you searched, for it
belonged to a gone-by time—a time now quite passed
away.

It stood in a street, but yet it was not like a town
house, for though the front opened right on to the pave-
ment the back windows looked out upon a beautiful,
quaintly terraced garden with old trees growing so
thick and close together that in summer it was like
living on the edge of a forest to be near them; and even
in winter the web of their interlaced branches hid all
clear view behind.

There was a colony of rooks in this old garden.
Year after year they held their parliaments and cawed
and chattered and fussed; year after year they built their
nests and hatched their eggs; year after year, I *suppose*,
the old ones gradually died off and the young ones
took their place, though, but for knowing this *must*
be so, no one would have suspected it, for to all appearance the rooks were always the same—ever and always
the same.

Time indeed seemed to stand still in and all about the old house, as if it and the people who inhabited it had got *so* old that they could not get any older, and had outlived the possibility of change.

But one day at last there did come a change. Late in the dusk of an autumn afternoon a carriage drove up to the door of the old house, came rattling over the stones with a sudden noisy clatter that sounded quite impertinent, startling the rooks just as they were composing themselves to rest, and setting them all wondering what could be the matter.

A little girl was the matter! A little girl in a grey merino frock and grey beaver bonnet, grey tippet and grey gloves—all grey together, even to her eyes, all except her round rosy face and bright brown hair. Her name even was rather grey, for it was Griselda.

A gentleman lifted her out of the carriage and disappeared with her into the house, and later that same evening the gentleman came out of the house and got into the carriage, which had come back for him again, and drove away. That was all that the rooks saw of the change that had come to the old house. Shall we go inside to see more?

Up the shallow, wide, old-fashioned staircase, past the wainscoted walls, dark and shining like a mirror, down a long narrow passage with many doors, which but for their gleaming brass handles one would not have known were there, the oldest of the three old servants led little Griselda, so tired and sleepy that her supper had been left almost untasted, to the room prepared for

Arriving

her.   It was a queer room, for everything in the house
was queer; but in the dancing light of the fire burning
brightly in the tiled grate, it looked cheerful enough.

'I am glad there's a fire,' said the child.   'Will it
keep alight till the morning, do you think?'

The old servant shook her head.

''Twould not be safe to leave it so that it would burn
till morning,' she said.   'When you are in bed and
asleep, little missie, you won't want the fire.   Bed's
the warmest place.'

'It isn't for that I want it,' said Griselda; 'it's for
the light I like it.   This house all looks so dark to me,
and yet there seem to be lights hidden in the walls too,
they shine so.'

The old servant smiled.

'It will all seem strange to you, no doubt,' she said;
'but you'll get to like it, missie.   'Tis a *good* old house,
and those that know best love it well.'

'Whom do you mean?' said Griselda.   'Do you
mean my great-aunts?'

'Ah, yes, and others beside,' replied the old woman.
'The rooks love it well, and others beside.   Did you
ever hear tell of the "good people," missie, over the
sea where you come from?'

'Fairies, do you mean?' cried Griselda, her eyes
sparkling.   'Of course I've *heard* of them, but I never
saw any.   Did you ever?'

'I couldn't say,' answered the old woman.   'My
mind is not young like yours, missie, and there are
times when strange memories come back to me as of

See page 50

. . . the mandarins on each side, nodding politely . . .

sights and sounds in a dream. I am too old to see and hear as I once could. We are all old here, missie. 'Twas time something young came to the old house again.'

'How strange and queer everything seems!' thought Griselda, as she got into bed. 'I don't feel as if I belonged to it a bit. And they are all *so* old; perhaps they won't like having a child among them?'

The very same thought that had occurred to the rooks! They could not decide as to the fors and againsts at all, so they settled to put it to the vote the next morning, and in the meantime they and Griselda all went to sleep.

I never heard if *they* slept well that night; after such unusual excitement it was hardly to be expected they would. But Griselda, being a little girl and not a rook, was so tired that two minutes after she had tucked herself up in bed she was quite sound asleep, and did not wake for several hours.

'I wonder what it will all look like in the morning,' was her last waking thought. 'If it was summer now, or spring, I shouldn't mind—there would always be something nice to do then.'

As sometimes happens, when she woke again very early in the morning, long before it was light, her thoughts went straight on with the same subject.

'If it was summer now, or spring,' she repeated to herself, just as if she had not been asleep at all—like the man who fell into a trance .for a hundred years just as he was saying 'it is bitt—' and when he woke

up again finished the sentence as if nothing had happened '—erly cold.' 'If only it was spring,' thought
Griselda.

Just as she had got so far in her thoughts she gave a
great start. What was it she heard? Could her wish
have come true? Was this fairyland indeed that she
had got to, where one only needs to *wish*, for it to *be*?
She rubbed her eyes, but it was too dark to see; *that*
was not very fairyland-like, but her ears she felt
certain had not deceived her: she was quite, quite sure
that she had heard the cuckoo!

She listened with all her might, but she did not hear
it again. Could it, after all, have been fancy? She
grew sleepy at last, and was just dropping off when—
yes, there it was again, as clear and distinct as possible:
'Cuckoo, cuckoo, cuckoo!' three, four, *five* times, then
perfect silence as before.

'What a funny cuckoo,' said Griselda to herself. 'I
could almost fancy it was in the house. I wonder if
my great-aunts have a tame cuckoo in a cage? I don't
think I ever heard of such a thing, but this is such a
queer house; everything seems different in it—perhaps
they have a tame cuckoo. I'll ask them in the morning. It's very nice to hear, whatever it is.'

And, with a pleasant feeling of companionship, a
sense that she was not the only living creature awake
in this dark world, Griselda lay listening, contentedly
enough, for the sweet, fresh notes of the cuckoo's
friendly greeting. But before it sounded again through
the silent house she was once more fast asleep. And

this time she slept till daylight had found its way into all but the *very* darkest nooks and crannies of the ancient dwelling.

She dressed herself carefully, for she had been warned that her aunts loved neatness and precision; she fastened each button of her grey frock, and tied down her hair as smooth as such a brown tangle *could* be tied down ; and, absorbed with these weighty cares, she forgot all about the cuckoo for the time. It was not till she was sitting at breakfast with her aunts that she remembered it, or rather was reminded of it, by some little remark that was made about the friendly robins on the terrace walk outside.

'Oh, aunt!' she exclaimed, stopping short half-way the journey to her mouth of a spoonful of bread and milk. 'Have you got a cuckoo in a cage?'

'A cuckoo in a cage,' repeated her elder aunt, Miss Grizzel. 'What is the child talking about?'

'In a cage!' echoed Miss Tabitha. 'A cuckoo in a cage!'

'There is a cuckoo somewhere in the house,' said Griselda. 'I heard it in the night. It couldn't have been out of doors, could it? It would be too cold.'

The aunts looked at each other with a little smile. 'So like her grandmother,' they whispered. Then said Miss Grizzel:

'We have a cuckoo, my dear, though it isn't in a cage, and it isn't exactly the sort of cuckoo you are thinking of. It lives in a clock.'

'In a clock,' repeated Miss Tabitha, as if to confirm her sister's statement.

B

'In a clock!' exclaimed Griselda, opening her grey eyes very wide.

It sounded something like the three bears, all speaking one after the other, only Griselda's voice was not like Tiny's; it was the loudest of the three.

'In a clock!' she exclaimed; 'but it can't be alive, then?'

'Why not?' said Miss Grizzel.

'I don't know,' replied Griselda, looking puzzled.

'I knew a little girl once,' pursued Miss Grizzel, 'who was quite of opinion the cuckoo *was* alive, and nothing would have persuaded her it was not.   Finish your breakfast, my dear, and then if you like you shall come with me and see the cuckoo for yourself.'

'Thank you, Aunt Grizzel,' said Griselda, going on with her bread and milk.

'Yes,' said Miss Tabitha, 'you shall see the cuckoo for yourself.'

'Thank you, Aunt Tabitha,' said Griselda.   It was rather a bother to have always to say 'thank you,' or 'no, thank you,' twice, but Griselda thought it was polite to do so, as Aunt Tabitha always repeated everything that Aunt Grizzel said.   It wouldn't have mattered so much if Aunt Tabitha had said it *at once* after Miss Grizzel, but as she generally made a little pause between, it was sometimes rather awkward.   But of course it was better to say 'thank you' or 'no, thank you' twice over than to hurt Aunt Tabitha's feelings.

After breakfast Aunt Grizzel was as good as her word. She took Griselda through several of the rooms in the house, pointing out all the curiosities, and telling all the histories of the rooms and their contents; and Griselda liked to listen, only in every room they came to she wondered *when* they would get to the room where lived the cuckoo.

Aunt Tabitha did not come with them, for she was rather rheumatic. On the whole, Griselda was not sorry. It would have taken such a *very* long time, you see, to have had all the histories twice over, and possibly, if Griselda had got tired, she might have forgotten about the 'thank yous' or 'no, thank yous' twice over.

The old house looked quite as queer and quaint by daylight as it had seemed the evening before; almost more so indeed, for the view from the windows added to the sweet, odd 'old-fashionedness' of everything.

'We have beautiful roses in summer,' observed Miss Grizzel, catching sight of the direction in which the child's eyes were wandering.

'I wish it was summer. I do love summer,' said Griselda. 'But there is a very rosy scent in the rooms even now, Aunt Grizzel, though it is winter, or nearly winter.'

Miss Grizzel looked pleased.

'My pot-pourri,' she explained.

They were just then standing in what she called the 'great saloon,' a handsome old room, furnished with gold-and-white chairs, that must once have been brilliant, and faded yellow damask hangings. A feeling of awe had crept over Griselda as they entered this ancient drawing-room. What grand parties there must

have been in it long ago! But as for dancing in it *now*
—dancing or laughing or chattering—such a thing
was quite impossible to imagine!

Miss Grizzel crossed the room to where stood in one
corner a marvellous Chinese cabinet, all black and
gold and carving. It was made in the shape of a
temple, or a palace—Griselda was not sure which. Any
way, it was very delicious and wonderful. At the
door stood, one on each side, two solemn mandarins;
or, to speak more correctly, perhaps I should say, a
mandarin and his wife, for the right-hand figure was
evidently intended to be a lady.

Miss Grizzel gently touched their heads. Forthwith,
to Griselda's astonishment, they began solemnly to
nod.

'Oh, how do you make them do that, Aunt Grizzel?'
she exclaimed.

'Never you mind, my dear; it wouldn't do for *you*
to try to make them nod. They wouldn't like it,'
replied Miss Grizzel mysteriously. 'Respect to your
elders, my dear, always remember that. The mandarins are *many* years older than you—older than I
myself, in fact.'

Griselda wondered, if this were so, how it was that
Miss Grizzel took such liberties with them herself,
but she said nothing.

'Here is my last summer's pot-pourri,' continued
Miss Grizzel, touching a great china jar on a little
stand, close beside the cabinet. 'You may smell it,
my dear.'

Nothing loath, Griselda buried her round little nose in the fragrant leaves.

'It's lovely,' she said. 'May I smell it whenever I like, Aunt Grizzel?'

'We shall see,' replied her aunt. 'It isn't *every* little girl, you know, that we could trust to come into the great saloon alone.'

'No,' said Griselda meekly.

Miss Grizzel led the way to a door opposite to that by which they had entered. She opened it and passed through, Griselda following, into a small ante-room.

'It is on the stroke of ten,' said Miss Grizzel, consulting her watch. 'Now, my dear, you shall make acquaintance with our cuckoo.'

The cuckoo 'that lived in a clock!' Griselda gazed round her eagerly. Where was the clock? She could see nothing in the least like one, only up on the wall in one corner was what looked like a miniature house, of dark brown carved wood. It was not so *very* like a house, but it certainly had a roof—a roof with deep projecting eaves; and, looking closer, yes, it *was* a clock, after all, only the figures, which had once been gilt, had grown dim with age, like everything else, and the hands at a little distance were hardly to be distinguished from the face.

Miss Grizzel stood perfectly still, looking up at the clock; Griselda beside her, in breathless expectation. Presently there came a sort of distant rumbling. *Something* was going to happen. Suddenly two little doors above the clock face, which Griselda had not known were there, sprang open with a burst and out flew a cuckoo, flapped his wings, and uttered his pretty cry: 'Cuckoo! cuckoo! cuckoo!' Miss Grizzel counted aloud, 'Seven, eight, nine, ten. Yes, he never makes a mistake,' she added triumphantly. 'All these long years I have never known him wrong. There are no such clocks made nowadays, I can assure you, my dear.'

'But *is* it a clock? Isn't he alive?' exclaimed Griselda. 'He looked at me and nodded his head, before he flapped his wings and went into his house again—he did indeed, aunt,' she said earnestly; 'just like saying "How do you do?" to me.'

Again Miss Grizzel smiled, the same odd yet pleased smile that Griselda had seen on her face at breakfast. 'Just what Sybilla used to say,' she murmured. 'Well, my dear,' she added aloud, 'it is quite right he *should* say "How do you do?" to you. It is the first time he has seen *you*, though many a year ago he knew your dear grandmother, and your father, too, when he was a little boy. You will find him a good friend, and one that can teach you many lessons.'

'What, Aunt Grizzel?' inquired Griselda, looking puzzled.

'Punctuality, for one thing, and faithful discharge of duty,' replied Miss Grizzel.

'May I come to see the cuckoo—to watch for him coming out, sometimes?' asked Griselda, who felt as if she could spend all day looking up at the clock, watching for her little friend's appearance.

'You will see him several times a day,' said her aunt,

'for it is in this little room I intend you to prepare your tasks. It is nice and quiet, and nothing to disturb you, and close to the room where your Aunt Tabitha and I usually sit.'

So saying, Miss Grizzel opened a second door in the little ante-room, and, to Griselda's surprise, at the foot of a short flight of stairs through another door, half open, she caught sight of her Aunt Tabitha, knitting quietly by the fire, in the room in which they had breakfasted.

'What a *very* funny house it is, Aunt Grizzel,' she said, as she followed her aunt down the steps. 'Every room has so many doors, and you come back to where you were just when you think you are ever so far off. I shall never be able to find my way about.'

'Oh yes, you will, my dear, very soon,' said her aunt encouragingly.

'She is very kind,' thought Griselda; 'but I wish she wouldn't call my lessons tasks. It makes them sound so dreadfully hard. But, any way, I'm glad I'm to do them in the room where that dear cuckoo lives.'

II

Impatient Griselda

. . . fairies but seldom appear;
If we do wrong we must expect
That it will cost us dear!

IT was all very well for a few days. Griselda found plenty to amuse herself with while the novelty lasted, enough to prevent her missing *very* badly the home she had left 'over the sea,' and the troop of noisy merry brothers who teased and petted her. Of course she *missed* them, but not 'dreadfully.' She was neither homesick nor 'dull.'

It was not quite such smooth sailing when lessons began. She did not dislike lessons; in fact, she had always thought she was rather fond of them. But the having to do them alone was not lively, and her teachers were very strict. The worst of all was the writing and arithmetic master, a funny little old man who wore

Mountains of figures

14

knee-breeches and took snuff, and called her aunt 'Madame,' bowing formally whenever he addressed her. He screwed Griselda up into such an unnatural attitude to write her copies, that she really felt as if she would never come straight and loose again; and the arith-metic part of his instructions was even worse. Oh! what sums in addition he gave her! Griselda had never been partial to sums, and her rather easy-going governess at home had not, to tell the truth, been partial to them either. And

Mr Kneebreeches

Mr—I can't remember the little old gentleman's name. Suppose we call him Mr Kneebreeches—Mr Knee-breeches, when he found this out, conscientiously put her back to the very beginning.

It was dreadful, really. He came twice a week, and the days he didn't come were as bad as those he did, for he left her a whole *row* I was going to say, but you couldn't call Mr Kneebreeches's addition sums 'rows,' they were far too fat and wide across to be so spoken of! —whole slatefuls of these terrible mountains of figures to climb wearily to the top of. And not to climb *once* up merely. *The* terrible thing was Mr Kneebreeches's favourite method of what he called 'proving.' I can't

explain it—it is far beyond my poor powers—but it had something to do with cutting off the top line, after you had added it all up and had actually done the sum, you understand—cutting off the top line and adding the long rows up again without it, and then joining it on again somewhere else.

'I wouldn't mind so much,' said poor Griselda, one day, 'if it was any good. But you see, Aunt Grizzel, it isn't. For I'm just as likely to do the *proving* wrong as the sum itself—more likely, for I'm always so tired when I get to the proving—and so all that's proved is that *something*'s wrong, and I'm sure that isn't any good, except to make me cross.'

'Hush!' said her aunt gravely. 'That is not the way for a little girl to speak. Improve these golden hours of youth, Griselda; they will never return.'

'I hope not,' muttered Griselda, 'if it means doing sums.'

Miss Grizzel fortunately was a little deaf; she did not hear this remark. Just then the cuckoo clock struck eleven.

'Good little cuckoo,' said Miss Grizzel. 'What an example he sets you. His life is spent in the faithful discharge of duty'; and so saying she left the room.

The cuckoo was still telling the hour—eleven took a good while. It seemed to Griselda that the bird repeated her aunt's last words. 'Faith—ful, dis—charge, of—your, du—ty,' he said, 'faith—ful.'

'You horrid little creature!' exclaimed Griselda in a passion. 'What business have you to mock me?'

She seized a book, the first that came to hand, and flung it at the bird, who was just beginning his eleventh cuckoo. He disappeared with a snap, disappeared without flapping his wings, or, as Griselda always fancied he did, giving her a friendly nod, and in an instant all was silent.

Griselda felt a little frightened. What had she done? She looked

'You horrid little creature!'

up at the clock.   It seemed just the same as usual, the cuckoo's doors closely shut, no sign of any disturbance. Could it have been her fancy only that he had sprung back more hastily than he would have done but for her throwing the book at him?   She began to hope so, and tried to go on with her lessons.   But it was no use.   Though she really gave her best attention to the long addition sums, and found that by so doing she managed them much better than before, she could not feel happy or at ease.   Every few minutes she glanced up at the clock, as if expecting the cuckoo to come out, though she knew quite well there was no chance of his doing so till twelve o'clock, as it was only the hours, not the half-hours and quarters, that he told.

'I wish it was twelve o'clock,' she said to herself anxiously more than once.

If only the clock had not been so very high up on the wall, she would have been tempted to climb up and open the little doors, and peep in to satisfy herself as to the cuckoo's condition.   But there was no possibility of this.   The clock was far, very far above her reach, and there was no high piece of furniture standing near, upon which she could have climbed to get to it. There was nothing to be done but to wait for twelve o'clock.

And, after all, she did not wait for twelve o'clock, for just about half-past eleven Miss Grizzel's voice was heard calling to her to put on her hat and cloak quickly, and come out to walk up and down the terrace with her.

'It is fine just now,' said Miss Grizzel, 'but there is a prospect of rain before long. You must leave your lessons for the present, and finish them in the afternoon.'

'I have finished them,' said Griselda meekly.

'*All?*' inquired her aunt.

'Yes, all,' replied Griselda.

'Ah, well, then, this afternoon, if the rain holds off, we shall drive to Merrybrow Hall, and inquire for the health of your dear godmother, Lady Lavander,' said Miss Grizzel.

Poor Griselda! There were few things she disliked more than a drive with her aunts. They went in the old yellow chariot, with all the windows up, and of course Griselda had to sit with her back to the horses, which made her very uncomfortable when she had no air, and had to sit still for so long.

Merrybrow Hall was a large house, quite as old and much grander, but not nearly so wonderful as the home of Griselda's aunts. It was six miles off, and it took a very long time indeed to drive there in the rumbling old chariot, for the old horses were fat and wheezy, and the old coachman fat and wheezy too. Lady Lavander was, of course, old too—very old indeed, and rather grumpy and very deaf. Miss Grizzel and Miss Tabitha had the greatest respect for her; she always called them 'My dear,' as if they were quite girls, and they listened to all she said as if her words were of gold. For some mysterious reason she had been invited to be Griselda's godmother; but, as she had never shown her any proof of affection beyond giving her a prayer book, and

The drive in the rumbling old chariot

hoping, whenever she saw her, that she was 'a good little miss,' Griselda did not feel any particular cause for gratitude to her.

The drive seemed longer and duller than ever this afternoon, but Griselda bore it meekly; and when Lady

Lavander, as usual, expressed her hopes about her, the little girl looked down modestly, feeling her cheeks grow scarlet. 'I am not a good little girl at all,' she felt inclined to call out. 'I'm very bad and cruel. I believe I've killed the dear little cuckoo.'

What *would* the three old ladies have thought if she had called it out? As it was, Lady Lavander patted her approvingly, said she loved to see young people modest and humble-minded, and gave her a slice of very highly spiced, rather musty gingerbread, which Griselda couldn't bear.

All the way home Griselda felt in a fever of impatience to rush up to the ante-room and see if the cuckoo was all right again. It was late and dark when the chariot at last stopped at the door of the old house. Miss Grizzel got out slowly, and still more slowly Miss Tabitha followed her. Griselda was obliged to restrain herself and move demurely.

'It is past your supper-time, my dear,' said Miss Grizzel. 'Go up at once to your room, and Dorcas shall bring some supper to you. Late hours are bad for young people.'

Griselda obediently wished her aunts good night, and went quietly upstairs. But once out of sight, at the first landing, she changed her pace. She turned to the left instead of to the right, which led to her own room, and flew rather than ran along the dimly lighted passage, at the end of which a door led into the great saloon. She opened the door. All was quite dark. It was impossible to fly or run across the great saloon! Even

in daylight this would have been a difficult matter.
Griselda *felt* her way as best she could, past the Chinese
cabinet and the pot-pourri jar, till she got to the ante-
room door.   It was open, and now, knowing her way
better, she hurried in.   But what was the use?   All
was silent, save the tick-tick of the cuckoo clock in the
corner.   Oh, if *only* the cuckoo would come out and
call the hour as usual, what a weight would be lifted off
Griselda's heart!

She had no idea what o'clock it was.   It might be
close to the hour, or it might be just past it.   She stood
listening for a few minutes, then hearing Miss Grizzel's
voice in the distance, she felt that she dared not stay
any longer, and turned to feel her way out of the room
again.   Just as she got to the door it seemed to her that
something softly brushed her cheek, and a very, very
faint 'cuckoo' sounded as it were in the air close to
her.

Startled, but not frightened, Griselda stood perfectly
still.

'Cuckoo,' she said softly.   But there was no
answer.

Again the tones of Miss Grizzel's voice coming
upstairs reached her ear.

'I *must* go,' said Griselda; and finding her way across
the saloon without, by great good luck, tumbling
against any of the many breakable treasures with which
it was filled, she flew down the long passage again, reaching her own room just before Dorcas appeared with
her supper.

Griselda slept badly that night.   She was constantly
dreaming of the cuckoo, fancying she heard his voice,
and then waking with a start to find it was *only* fancy.
She looked pale and heavy-eyed when she came down
to breakfast the next morning; and her Aunt Tabitha,
who was alone in the room when she entered, began
immediately asking her what was the matter.

'I am sure you are going to be ill, child,' she said
nervously. 'Sister Grizzel must give you some medi-
cine.   I wonder what would be the best.   Tansy tea
is an excellent thing when one has taken cold, or——'

But the rest of Miss Tabitha's sentence was never
heard, for at this moment Miss Grizzel came hurriedly
into the room—her cap awry, her shawl disarranged,
her face very pale.   I hardly think anyone had ever
seen her so discomposed before.

'Sister Tabitha!' she exclaimed, 'what can be going
to happen?   The cuckoo clock has stopped.'

'The cuckoo clock has stopped!' repeated Miss
Tabitha, holding up her hands.   '*Im*possible!'

'But it has, or rather I should say—dear me, I am
so upset I cannot explain myself—the *cuckoo* has
stopped.   The clock is going on, but the cuckoo has
not told the hours, and Dorcas is of opinion that he left
off doing so yesterday.   What can be going to happen?
What shall we do?'

'What can we do?' said Miss Tabitha.   'Should we
send for the watch-maker?'

Miss Grizzel shook her head.

''Twould be worse than useless.   Were we to search

c

the world over we could find no one to put it right. Fifty years and more, Tabitha, fifty years and more, it has never missed an hour! We are getting old, Tabitha, our day is nearly over; perhaps 'tis to remind us of this.'

Miss Tabitha did not reply. She was weeping silently. The old ladies seemed to have forgotten the presence of their niece, but Griselda could not bear to see their distress. She finished her breakfast as quickly as she could, and left the room.

On her way upstairs she met Dorcas.

'Have you heard what has happened, little missie?' said the old servant.

'Yes,' replied Griselda.

'My ladies are in great trouble,' continued Dorcas, who seemed inclined to be more communicative than usual, 'and no wonder. For fifty years that clock has never gone wrong.'

'Can't it be put right?' asked the child.

Dorcas shook her head.

'No good would come of interfering,' she said. 'What must be, must be. The luck of the house hangs on that clock. Its maker spent a good part of his life over it, and his last words were that it would bring good luck to the house that owned it, but that trouble would follow its silence. It's my belief,' she added solemnly, 'that it's a *fairy* clock, neither more or less, for good luck it has brought there's no denying. There are no cows like ours, missie—their milk is a proverb hereabouts; there are no hens like ours for laying all the year round; there are no roses like ours. And there's always a friendly feeling in this house, and always has been. 'Tis not a house for wrangling and jangling and sharp words. The "good people" can't stand that. Nothing drives them away like ill temper or anger.'

Griselda's conscience gave her a sharp prick. Could it be *her* doing that trouble was coming upon the old house? What a punishment for a moment's fit of ill temper.

'I wish you wouldn't talk that way, Dorcas,' she said, 'it makes me so unhappy.'

'What a feeling heart the child has,' said the old servant as she went on her way downstairs. 'It's true —she is very like Miss Sybilla.'

That day was a very weary and sad one for Griselda. She was oppressed by a feeling she did not understand. She knew she had done wrong, but she had sorely repented it, and 'I do think the cuckoo might have come back again,' she said to herself, 'if he *is* a fairy; and if he isn't, it can't be true what Dorcas says.'

Her aunts made no allusion to the subject in her presence, and almost seemed to have forgotten that she had known of their distress. They were more grave and silent than usual, but otherwise things went on in their ordinary way. Griselda spent the morning 'at her tasks,' in the ante-room, but was thankful to get away from the tick-tick of the clock in the corner and out into the garden.

But there, alas! it was just as bad. The rooks seemed

to know that something was the matter; they set to work making such a chatter immediately Griselda appeared that she felt inclined to run back into the house again.

'I am sure they are talking about me,' she said to herself. 'Perhaps they are fairies too. I am beginning to think I don't like fairies.'

She was glad when bedtime came. It was a sort of reproach to her to see her aunts so pale and troubled; and though she tried to persuade herself that she thought them very silly, she could not throw off the uncomfortable feeling.

She was so tired when she went to bed—tired in the disagreeable way that comes from a listless, uneasy day —that she fell asleep at once and slept heavily. When she woke, which she did suddenly, and with a start, it was still perfectly dark, like the first morning that she had wakened in the old house. It seemed to her that she had not wakened of herself—something had roused her. Yes! there it was again, a very, *very* soft distant 'cuckoo.' *Was* it distant? She could not tell. Almost she could have fancied it was close to her.

'If it's that cuckoo come back again, I'll catch him!' exclaimed Griselda.

She darted out of bed, felt her way to the door, which was closed, and opening it let in a rush of moonlight from the unshuttered passage window. In another moment her little bare feet were pattering along the passage at full speed, in the direction of the great saloon.

For Griselda's childhood among the troop of noisy brothers had taught her one lesson—she was afraid of nothing.   Or rather perhaps I should say she had never learnt that there was anything to be afraid of!   And is there?

III

Obeying Orders

Little girl, thou must thy part fulfil,
If we're to take kindly to ours:
Then pull up the weeds with a will,
And fairies will cherish the flowers.

THERE was moonlight, though not so much, in the saloon and the ante-room, too; for though the windows, like those in Griselda's bedroom, had the shutters closed, there was a round part at the top, high up, which the shutters did not reach to, and in crept, through these clear uncovered panes, quite as many moonbeams, you may be sure, as could find their way.

Griselda, eager though she was, could not help standing still a moment to admire the effect.

'It looks prettier with the light coming in at those holes at the top than even if the shutters were open,' she said to herself. 'How goldy-silvery the cabinet looks; and, yes, I do declare, the mandarins are nodding! I wonder if it is out of politeness to me, or does Aunt Grizzel come in last thing at night and touch them to make them keep nodding till morning? I *suppose* they're a sort of policemen to the palace; and I dare say there are all sorts of beautiful things inside. How I should like to see all through it!'

But at this moment the faint tick-tick of the cuckoo

28

clock in the next room, reaching her ear, reminded her of the object of this midnight expedition of hers. She hurried into the ante-room.

It looked darker than the great saloon, for it had but one window. But through the uncovered space at the top of this window there penetrated some brilliant moonbeams, one of which lighted up brightly the face of the clock with its queer overhanging eaves.

Griselda approached it and stood below, looking up.

'Cuckoo,' she said softly—very softly.

But there was no reply.

'Cuckoo,' she repeated rather more loudly. 'Why won't you speak to me? I know you are there, and you're not asleep, for I heard your voice in my own room. Why won't you come out, cuckoo?'

'Tick-tick,' said the clock, but there was no other reply.

Griselda felt ready to cry.

'Cuckoo,' she said reproachfully, 'I didn't think you were so hard-hearted. I have been *so* unhappy about you, and I was so pleased to hear your voice again, for I thought I had killed you, or hurt you very badly; and I didn't *mean* to hurt you, cuckoo. I was sorry the moment I had done it, *dreadfully* sorry. Dear cuckoo, won't you forgive me?'

There was a little sound at last—a faint *coming* sound, and by the moonlight Griselda saw the doors open, and out flew the cuckoo. He stood still for a moment, looked round him as it were, then gently flapped his wings, and uttered his usual note: 'Cuckoo.'

Griselda stood in breathless expectation, but in her delight she could not help very softly clapping her hands.

The cuckoo cleared his throat. You never heard such a funny little noise as he made; and then, in a very clear, distinct, but yet 'cuckoo-y' voice, he spoke.

'Griselda,' he said, 'are you truly sorry?'

'I told you I was,' she replied. 'But I didn't *feel* so very naughty, cuckoo. I didn't, really. I was only vexed for one minute, and when I threw the book I seemed to be a very little in fun, too. And it made me so unhappy when you went away, and my poor aunts have been dreadfully unhappy too. If you hadn't come back I should have told them to-morrow what I had done. I would have told them before, but I was afraid it would have made them more unhappy. I thought I had hurt you dreadfully.'

'So you did,' said the cuckoo.

'But you *look* quite well,' said Griselda.

'It was my *feelings*,' replied the cuckoo; 'and I couldn't help going away. I have to obey orders like other people.'

Griselda stared. 'How do you mean?' she asked.

'Never mind. You can't understand at present,' said the cuckoo. 'You can understand about obeying *your* orders, and you see, when you don't, things go wrong.'

'Yes,' said Griselda humbly, 'they certainly do. But, cuckoo,' she continued, 'I never used to get into tempers at home—*hardly* never, at least; and I liked my lessons then, and I never was scolded about them.'

'Why won't you speak to me?'

'What's wrong here, then?' said the cuckoo. 'It isn't often that things go wrong in this house.'

'That's what Dorcas says,' said Griselda. 'It must be with my being a child—my aunts and the house and everything have got out of children's ways.'

'About time they did,' remarked the cuckoo dryly.

'And so,' continued Griselda, 'it is really very dull. I have lots of lessons, but it isn't so much that I mind. It is that I've no one to play with.'

'There's something in that,' said the cuckoo. He flapped his wings and was silent for a minute or two. 'I'll consider about it,' he observed at last.

'Thank you,' said Griselda, not exactly knowing what else to say.

'And in the meantime,' continued the cuckoo, 'you'd better obey present orders and go back to bed.'

'Shall I say good night to you, then?' asked Griselda somewhat timidly.

'You're quite welcome to do so,' replied the cuckoo. 'Why shouldn't you?'

'You see, I wasn't sure if you would like it,' returned Griselda, 'for of course you're not like a person, and—and—I've been told all sorts of queer things about what fairies like and don't like.'

'Who said I was a fairy?' inquired the cuckoo.

'Dorcas did, and, *of course*, my own common sense did too,' replied Griselda. 'You must be a fairy—you couldn't be anything else.'

'I might be a fairyfied cuckoo,' suggested the bird.

Griselda looked puzzled.

'I don't understand,' she said, 'and I don't think it could make much difference. But whatever you are, I wish you would tell me one thing.'

'What?' said the cuckoo.

'I want to know, now that you've forgiven me for throwing the book at you, have you come back for good?'

'Certainly not for evil,' replied the cuckoo.

Griselda gave a little wriggle. 'Cuckoo, you're laughing at me,' she said. 'I mean, have you come back to stay and cuckoo as usual and make my aunts happy again?'

'You'll see in the morning,' said the cuckoo. 'Now go off to bed.'

'Good night,' said Griselda, 'and thank you, and please don't forget to let me know when you've considered.'

'Cuckoo, cuckoo,' was her little friend's reply. Griselda thought it was meant for good night, but the fact of the matter was that at that exact second of time it was two o'clock in the morning.

She made her way back to bed. She had been standing some time talking to the cuckoo, but, though it was now well on in November, she did not feel the least cold, nor sleepy! She felt as happy and light-hearted as possible, and she wished it was morning, that she might get up. Yet the moment she laid her little brown curly head on the pillow she fell asleep; and it seemed to her that just as she dropped off a soft feathery wing brushed her cheek gently and a tiny 'Cuckoo' sounded in her ear.

When she woke it was bright morning, really bright morning, for the wintry sun was already sending some clear yellow rays out into the pale grey-blue sky.

'It must be late,' thought Griselda, when she had opened the shutters and seen how light it was. 'I must have slept a long time. I feel so beautifully unsleepy now. I must dress quickly—how nice it will be to see my aunts look happy again! I don't even care if they scold me for being late.'

But, after all, it was not so much later than usual; it was only a much brighter morning than they had had for some time. Griselda did dress herself very quickly, however. As she went downstairs two or three of the clocks in the house, for there were several, were striking eight. These clocks must have been a little before the right time, for it was not till they had again relapsed into silence that there rang out from the ante-room the clear sweet tones, eight times repeated, of 'Cuckoo.'

Miss Grizzel and Miss Tabitha were already at the breakfast-table, but they received their little niece most graciously. Nothing was said about the clock, however, till about half-way through the meal, when Griselda, full of eagerness to know if her aunts were aware of the cuckoo's return, could restrain herself no longer.

'Aunt Grizzel,' she said, 'isn't the cuckoo all right again?'

'Yes, my dear. I am delighted to say it is,' replied Miss Grizzel.

'Did you get it put right, Aunt Grizzel?' inquired Griselda slyly.

'Little girls should not ask so many questions,' replied Miss Grizzel mysteriously. It *is* all right again, and that is enough. During fifty years that cuckoo has never, till yesterday, missed an hour. If you, in your sphere, my dear, do as well during fifty years, you won't have done badly.'

'No, indeed, you won't have done badly,' repeated Miss Tabitha.

But though the two old ladies thus tried to improve the occasion by a little lecturing, Griselda could see that at the bottom of their hearts they were both so happy that, even if she had been very naughty indeed, they could hardly have made up their minds to scold her.

She was not at all inclined to be naughty this day. She had something to think about and look forward to, which made her quite a different little girl, and made her take heart in doing her lessons as well as she possibly could.

'I wonder when the cuckoo will have considered enough about my having no one to play with?' she said to herself, as she was walking up and down the terrace at the back of the house.

'Caw, caw!' screamed a rook just over her head, as if in answer to her thought.

Griselda looked up at him.

'Your voice isn't half so pretty as the cuckoo's, Mr Rook,' she said. 'All the same, I dare say I should make friends with you, if I understood what you meant. How funny it would be to know all the languages of the

birds and the beasts, like the prince in the fairy-tale!
I wonder if I should wish for that, if a fairy gave me a
wish? No, I don't think I would. I'd *far* rather
have the fairy carpet that would take you anywhere you
liked in a minute. I'd go to China to see if all the
people there look like Aunt Grizzel's mandarins; and
I'd first of all, of course, go to fairyland.'

'You must come in now, little missie,' said Dorcas's
voice. 'Miss Grizzel says you have had play enough,
and there's a nice fire in the ante-room for you to do
your lessons by.'

'Play!' repeated Griselda indignantly, as she turned
to follow the old servant. 'Do you call walking up and
down the terrace "play," Dorcas? I mustn't loiter
even to pick a flower, if there were any, for fear of
catching cold, and I mustn't run for fear of overheating
myself. I declare, Dorcas, if I don't have some play
soon, or something to amuse me, I think I'll run away.'

'Nay, nay, missie, don't talk like that. You'd never
do anything so naughty, and you so like Miss Sybilla,
who was so good.'

'Dorcas, I'm tired of being told I'm like Miss
Sybilla,' said Griselda impatiently. 'She was my
grandmother; no one would like to be told they were
like their grandmother. It makes me feel as if my
face must be all screwy up and wrinkly, and as if I
should have spectacles on and a wig.'

'*That* is not like what Miss Sybilla was when I first
saw her,' said Dorcas. 'She was younger than you,
missie, and as pretty as a fairy.'

'*Was* she?' exclaimed Griselda, stopping short.

'Yes, indeed she was. She might have been a fairy, so sweet she was and gentle—and yet so merry. Every creature loved her; even the animals about seemed to know her, as if she was one of themselves. She brought good luck to the house, and it was a sad day when she left it.'

'I thought you said it was the cuckoo that brought good luck?' said Griselda.

'Well, so it was. The cuckoo and Miss Sybilla came here the same day. It was left to her by her mother's father, with whom she had lived since she was a baby, and when he died she came here to her sisters. She wasn't *own* sister to my ladies, you see, missie. Her mother had come from Germany, and it was in some strange place there, where her grandfather lived, that the cuckoo clock was made. They make wonderful clocks there, I've been told, but none more wonderful than our cuckoo, I'm sure.'

'No, I'm *sure* not,' said Griselda softly. 'Why didn't Miss Sybilla take it with her when she was married and went away?

'She knew her sisters were so fond of it. It was like a memory of her left behind for them. It was like a part of her. And do you know, missie, the night she died—she died soon after your father was born, a year after she was married—for a whole hour, from twelve to one, that cuckoo went on cuckooing in a soft, sad way, like some living creature in trouble. Of course, we did not know anything was wrong with her, and

folks said something had caught some of the springs
of the works; but *I* didn't think so, and never shall.
And——'

But here Dorcas's reminiscences were abruptly
brought to a close by Miss Grizzel's appearance at the
other end of the terrace.

'Griselda, what are you loitering so for? Dorcas,
you should have hastened, not delayed Miss Griselda.'

So Griselda was hurried off to her lessons, and Dorcas
to her kitchen. But Griselda did not much mind.
She had plenty to think of and wonder about, and she
liked to do her lessons in the ante-room, with the tick-
tick of the clock in her ears, and the feeling that *perhaps*
the cuckoo was watching her through some invisible
peep-hole in his closed doors.

'And if he sees,' thought Griselda, 'if he sees how
hard I am trying to do my lessons well, it will perhaps
make him be quick about "considering."'

So she did try very hard. And she didn't speak to
the cuckoo when he came out to say it was four o'clock.
She was busy, and he was busy. She felt it was better
to wait till he gave her some sign of being ready to
talk to her again.

For fairies, you know, children, however charming,
are sometimes *rather* queer to have to do with. They
don't like to be interfered with, or treated except with
very great respect, and they have their own ideas about
what is proper and what isn't, I can assure you.

I suppose it was with working so hard at her lessons
—most people would say it was with having been up

the night before, running about the house in the moonlight; but as she had never felt so 'fresh' in her life as
when she got up that morning, it could hardly have
been that—that Griselda felt so tired and sleepy that
evening, she could hardly keep her eyes open. She
begged to go to bed quite half an hour earlier than
usual, which made Miss Tabitha afraid again that she
was going to be ill. But as there is nothing better for
children than to go to bed early, even if they *are* going
to be ill, Miss Grizzel told her to say good night, and
to ask Dorcas to give her a wineglassful of elderberry
wine, nice and hot, after she was in bed.

Griselda had no objection to the elderberry wine,
though she felt she was having it on false pretences.
She certainly did not need it to send her to sleep, for
almost before her head touched the pillow she was as
sound as a top. She had slept a good long while, when
again she wakened suddenly—just as she had done the
night before, and again with the feeling that something
had wakened her. And the queer thing was that the
moment she was awake she felt so *very* awake—she had
no inclination to stretch and yawn and hope it wasn't
quite time to get up, and think how nice and warm bed
was, and how cold it was outside! She sat straight up,
and peered out into the darkness, feeling quite ready
for an adventure.

'Is it you, cuckoo?' she said softly.

There was no answer, but listening intently, the
child fancied she heard a faint rustling or fluttering in
the corner of the room by the door. She got up and,

D

feeling her way, opened it, and the instant she had done so she heard, a few steps only in front of her it seemed, the familiar notes, very, *very* soft and whispered: 'Cuckoo, cuckoo.'

It went on and on, down the passage, Griselda trotting after. There was no moon to-night, heavy clouds had quite hidden it, and outside the rain was falling heavily. Griselda could hear it on the window-panes, through the closed shutters and all. But dark as it was, she made her way along without any difficulty, down the passage, across the great saloon, in through the ante-room door, guided only by the little voice now and then to be heard in front of her. She came to a standstill right before the clock, and stood there for a minute or two patiently waiting.

She had not very long to wait. There came the usual murmuring sound, then the doors above the clock face opened—she heard them open, it was far too dark to see—and in his ordinary voice, clear and distinct (it was just two o'clock, so the cuckoo was killing two birds with one stone, telling the hour and greeting Griselda at once), the bird sang out: 'Cuckoo, cuckoo.'

'Good evening, cuckoo,' said Griselda, when he had finished.

'Good morning, you mean,' said the cuckoo.

'Good morning, then, cuckoo,' said Griselda. 'Have you considered about me, cuckoo?'

The cuckoo cleared his throat.

'Have you learnt to obey orders yet, Griselda?' he inquired.

'I'm trying,' replied Griselda. 'But you see, cuckoo, I've not had very long to learn in—it was only last night you told me, you know.'

The cuckoo sighed.

'You've a great deal to learn, Griselda.'

'I dare say I have,' she said. 'But I can tell you one thing, cuckoo—whatever lessons I have, I *couldn't* ever have any worse than those addition sums of Mr Knee-breeches's. I have made up my mind about that, for to-day, do you know, cuckoo——'

'Yesterday,' corrected the cuckoo. 'Always be exact in your statements, Griselda.'

'Well, yesterday, then,' said Griselda rather tartly. 'Though when you know quite well what I mean, I don't see that you need be so *very* particular. Well, as I was saying, I tried and *tried*, but still they were fearful. They were, indeed.'

'You've a great deal to learn, Griselda,' repeated the cuckoo.

'I wish you wouldn't say that so often,' said Griselda. 'I thought you were going to *play* with me.'

'There's something in that,' said the cuckoo, 'there's something in that. I should like to talk about it. But we could talk more comfortably if you would come up here and sit beside me.'

Griselda thought her friend must be going out of his mind.

'Sit beside you up there!' she exclaimed. 'Cuckoo, how *could* I? I'm far, far too big.'

'Big!' returned the cuckoo. 'What do you mean by big? It's all a matter of fancy. Don't you know that if the world and every-thing in it, counting yourself, of course, was all made little enough to go into a walnut, you'd never find out the difference.'

'*Wouldn't* I?' said Griselda, feeling rather muddled; 'but, *not* counting myself, cuckoo, I would then, wouldn't I?'

'Nonsense,' said the cuckoo hastily; 'you've a great deal to learn, and one thing is, not to *argue*. Nobody should argue; it's a shocking bad habit, and ruins the digestion. Come up here and sit beside me comfort-

ably. Catch hold of the chain; you'll find you can manage if you try.'

'But it'll stop the clock,' said Griselda. 'Aunt Grizzel said I was never to touch the weights or the chains.'

'Stuff,' said the cuckoo; 'it won't stop the clock. Catch hold of the chains and swing yourself up. There now—I told you you could manage it.'

'Catch hold of the chains and swing yourself up'

IV

The Country of the Nodding Mandarins

We're all nodding, nid-nid-nodding.

How she managed it she never knew; but, somehow or other, it *was* managed. She seemed to slide up the chain just as easily as in a general way she would have slidden down, only without any disagreeable anticipation of a bump at the end of the journey. And when she got to the top how wonderfully different it looked from anything she could have expected! The doors stood open, and Griselda found them quite big enough, or herself quite small enough—which it was she couldn't tell, and as it was all a matter of fancy she decided not to trouble to inquire—to pass through quite comfortably.

And inside there was the most charming little snuggery imaginable. It was something like a saloon railway carriage—it seemed to be all lined and carpeted and everything, with rich mossy red velvet; there was a little round table in the middle and two arm-chairs, on one of which sat the cuckoo—'quite like other people,' thought Griselda to herself—while the other, as he pointed out to Griselda by a little nod, was evidently intended for her.

'Thank you,' said she, sitting down on the chair as she spoke.

43

'Are you comfortable?' inquired the cuckoo.

'Quite,' replied Griselda, looking about her with great satisfaction. 'Are all cuckoo clocks like this when you get up inside them?' she inquired. 'I can't think how there's room for this dear little place between the clock and the wall. Is it a hole cut out of the wall on purpose, cuckoo?'

'Hush!' said the cuckoo. 'We've got other things to talk about. First, shall I lend you one of my mantles? You may feel cold.'

'I don't just now,' replied Griselda, 'but perhaps I *might*.'

She looked at her little bare feet as she spoke, and wondered why *they* weren't cold, for it was very chilblainy weather.

The cuckoo stood up, and with one of his claws reached from a corner where it was hanging a cloak which Griselda had not before noticed. For it was hanging wrong side out, and the lining was red velvet, very like what the sides of the little room were covered with, so it was no wonder she had not noticed it.

Had it been hanging the *right* side out she must have done so; this side was so very wonderful!

It was all feathers—feathers of every shade and colour, but beautifully worked in, somehow, so as to lie quite smoothly and evenly, one colour melting away into another like those in a prism, so that you could hardly tell where one began and another ended.

'What a *lovely* cloak!' said Griselda, wrapping it round her and feeling even more comfortable than before, as she watched the rays of the little lamp in the roof—I think I was forgetting to tell you that the cuckoo's boudoir was lighted by a dear little lamp set into the red velvet roof like a pearl in a ring—playing softly on the brilliant colours of the feather mantle.

'It's better than lovely,' said the cuckoo, 'as you shall see.   Now, Griselda,' he continued, in the tone of one coming to business.   'Now, Griselda, let us talk.'

'We have been talking,' said Griselda, 'ever so long. I am very comfortable.   When you say "let us talk" like that, it makes me forget all I wanted to say.   Just let me sit still and say whatever comes into my head.'

'That won't do,' said the cuckoo; 'we must have a plan of action.'

'A what?' said Griselda.

'You see you *have* a great deal to learn,' said the cuckoo triumphantly.   'You don't understand what I say.'

'But I didn't come up here to learn,' said Griselda; 'I can do that down there'; and she nodded her head in the direction of the ante-room table.   'I want to play.'

'Just so,' said the cuckoo; 'that's what I want to talk about.   What do you call "play"—blind-man's-buff and that sort of thing?'

'No,' said Griselda, considering.   'I'm getting rather too big for that kind of play.   Besides, cuckoo, you and I alone couldn't have much fun at blind-man's-buff; there'd be only me to catch you or you to catch me.'

'Oh, we could easily get more,' said the cuckoo. 'The mandarins would be pleased to join.'

'The mandarins!' repeated Griselda. 'Why, cuckoo, they're not alive! How could they play?'

The cuckoo looked at her gravely for a minute, then shook his head.

'You have a *great* deal to learn,' he said solemnly. 'Don't you know that *everything*'s alive?'

'No,' said Griselda, 'I don't; and I don't know what you mean, and I don't think I want to know what you mean. I want to talk about playing.'

'Well,' said the cuckoo, 'talk.'

'What I call playing,' pursued Griselda, 'is—I have thought about it now, you see—is being amused. If you will amuse me, cuckoo, I will count that you are playing with me.'

'How shall I amuse you?' inquired he.

'Oh, that's for you to find out!' exclaimed Griselda. 'You might tell me fairy stories, you know: if you're a fairy you should know lots; or—oh yes, of course that would be far nicer—if you are a fairy you might take me with you to fairyland.'

Again the cuckoo shook his head.

'That,' said he, 'I cannot do.'

'Why not?' said Griselda. 'Lots of children have been there.'

'I doubt it,' said the cuckoo. '*Some* may have been, but not lots. And some may have thought they had been there who hadn't really been there at all. And as to those who have been there, you may be sure of one thing—they were not *taken*, they found their own way. No one ever was *taken* to fairyland—to the real fairyland. They may have been taken to the neighbouring countries, but not to fairyland itself.'

'And how is one ever to find one's own way there?' asked Griselda.

'That I cannot tell you, either,' replied the cuckoo. 'There are many roads there; you may find yours some day. And if ever you do find it, be sure you keep what you see of it well swept and clean, and then you may see further after a while. Ah, yes, there are many roads and many doors into fairyland!'

'Doors!' cried Griselda. 'Are there any doors into fairyland in this house?'

'Several,' said the cuckoo; 'but don't waste your time looking for them at present. It would be no use.'

'Then how will you amuse me?' inquired Griselda in a rather disappointed tone.

'Don't you care to go anywhere except to fairyland?' said the cuckoo.

'Oh yes, there are lots of places I wouldn't mind seeing. Not geography sort of places—it would be just like lessons to go to India and Africa and all those places—but *queer* places, like the mines where the goblins make diamonds and precious stones, and the caves down under the sea where the mermaids live. And—oh, I've just thought—now I'm so nice and little, I *would* like to go all over the mandarins' palace in the great saloon.'

'That can be easily managed,' said the cuckoo; 'but —excuse me for an instant,' he exclaimed suddenly.

He gave a spring forward and disappeared. Then Griselda heard his voice outside the doors: 'Cuckoo, cuckoo, cuckoo.' It was three o'clock.

The doors opened again to let him through, and he resettled himself on his chair. 'As I was saying,' he went on, 'nothing could be easier. But that palace, as you call it, has an entrance on the other side, as well as the one you know.'

'Another door, do you mean?' said Griselda. 'How funny! Does it go through the wall? And where does it lead to?'

'It leads,' replied the cuckoo, 'it leads to the country of the Nodding Mandarins.'

'*What* fun!' exclaimed Griselda, clapping her hands. 'Cuckoo, do let us go there. How can we get down? You can fly, but must I slide down the chain again?'

'Oh dear, no,' said the cuckoo, 'by no means. You have only to stretch out your feather mantle, flap it as if it was wings—so'—he flapped his own wings encouragingly—'wish, and there you'll be.'

'Where?' said Griselda bewilderedly.

'Wherever you wish to be, of course,' said the cuckoo. 'Are you ready? Here goes.'

'Wait—wait a moment,' cried Griselda. 'Where am I to wish to be?'

'Bless the child!' exclaimed the cuckoo. 'Where *do* you wish to be? You said you wanted to visit the country of the Nodding Mandarins.'

'Yes; but am I to wish first to be in the palace in the great saloon?'

'Certainly,' replied the cuckoo. 'That is the entrance to Mandarin Land, and you said you would like to see through it. So—you're surely ready now?'

'A thought has just struck me,' said Griselda. 'How will you know what o'clock it is, so as to come back in time to tell the next hour? My aunts will get into such a fright if you go wrong again! Are you sure we shall have time to go to the mandarins' country to-night?'

'Time!' repeated the cuckoo. 'What is time? Ah, Griselda, you have a *very* great deal to learn! What do you mean by time?'

'I don't know,' replied Griselda, feeling rather snubbed. 'Being slow or quick—I suppose that's what I mean.'

'And what is slow, and what is quick?' said the cuckoo. '*All* a matter of fancy! If everything that's been done since the world was made till now, was done over again in five minutes, you'd never know the difference.'

'Oh, cuckoo, I wish you wouldn't!' cried poor Griselda; 'you're worse than sums, you do so puzzle me. It's like what you said about nothing being big or little, only it's worse. Where would all the days and hours be if there was nothing but minutes? Oh, cuckoo, you said you'd amuse me, and you do nothing but puzzle me.'

'It was your own fault. You wouldn't get ready,' said the cuckoo. '*Now*, here goes! Flap and wish.'

Griselda flapped and wished. She felt a sort of rustle in the air, that was all—then she found herself standing with the cuckoo in front of the Chinese cabinet, the door of which stood open, while the mandarins on each side, nodding politely, seemed to invite them to enter. Griselda hesitated.

'Go on,' said the cuckoo patronizingly; 'ladies first.'

Griselda went on.   To her surprise, inside the cabinet it was quite light, though where the light came from that illuminated all the queer corners and recesses and streamed out to the front, where stood the mandarins, she could not discover.

The 'palace' was not quite as interesting as she had expected.   There were lots of little rooms in it opening on to balconies commanding, no doubt, a splendid view of the great saloon; there were ever so many little staircases leading to more little rooms and balconies; but it all seemed empty and deserted.

'I don't care for it,' said Griselda, stopping short at last; 'it's all the same, and there's nothing to see.   I thought my aunts kept ever so many beautiful things in here, and there's nothing.'

'Come along, then,' said the cuckoo.   'I didn't expect you'd care for the palace, as you called it, much. Let us go out the other way.'

He hopped down a sort of little staircase near which they were standing, and Griselda followed him willingly enough.   At the foot they found themselves in a vestibule, much handsomer than the entrance at the other side, and the cuckoo, crossing it, lifted one of his claws and touched a spring in the wall.   Instantly a pair of large doors flew open in the middle, revealing to

Griselda the prettiest and most curious sight she had
ever seen.

A flight of wide, shallow steps led down from this
doorway into a long, long avenue bordered by stiffly

He flapped his wings and instantly a palanquin appeared

growing trees, from the branches of which hung in-
numerable lamps of every colour, making a perfect
network of brilliance as far as the eye could reach.

'Oh, how lovely!' cried Griselda, clapping her hands.
'It'll be like walking along a rainbow. Cuckoo, come
quick.'

'Stop,' said the cuckoo; 'we've a good way to go.
There's no need to walk. Palanquin!'

He flapped his wings and instantly a palanquin
appeared at the foot of the steps. It was made of
carved ivory, and borne by four Chinese-looking figures

with pigtails and bright-coloured jackets. A feeling
came over Griselda that she was dreaming, or else that
she had seen this palanquin before. She hesitated.
Suddenly she gave a little jump of satisfaction.

'I know,' she exclaimed. 'It's exactly like the one
that stands under a glass shade on Lady Lavander's
drawing-room mantelpiece. I wonder if it is the very
one? Fancy me being able to get *into* it!'

She looked at the four bearers. Instantly they all
nodded.

'What do they mean?' asked Griselda, turning to
the cuckoo.

'Get in,' he replied.

'Yes, I'm just going to get in,' she said; 'but what
do *they* mean when they nod at me like that?'

'They mean, of course, what I tell you—"Get in,"'
said the cuckoo.

'Why don't they say so, then?' persisted Griselda,
getting in, however, as she spoke.

'Griselda, you have a *very* great——' began the
cuckoo, but Griselda interrupted him.

'Cuckoo,' she exclaimed, 'if you say that again, I'll
jump out of the palanquin and run away home to bed.
Of course I've a great deal to learn—that's why I like
to ask questions about everything I see. Now, tell me
where we are going.'

'In the first place,' said the cuckoo, 'are you comfortable?'

'Very,' said Griselda, settling herself down among
the cushions.

It was a change from the cuckoo's boudoir. There were no chairs or seats, only a number of very, *very* soft cushions covered with green silk. There were green silk curtains all round, too, which you could draw or not as you pleased, just by touching a spring. Griselda stroked the silk gently. It was not 'fruzzly' silk, if you know what that means; it did not make you feel as if your nails wanted cutting, or as if all the rough places on your skin were being rubbed up the wrong way; its softness was like that of a rose or pansy petal.

'What nice silk!' said Griselda. 'I'd like a dress of it. I never noticed that the palanquin was lined so nicely,' she continued, 'for I suppose it *is* the one from Lady Lavander's mantelpiece? There couldn't be two so exactly like each other.'

The cuckoo gave a sort of whistle.

'What a goose you are, my dear!' he exclaimed. 'Excuse me,' he continued, seeing that Griselda looked rather offended; 'I didn't mean to hurt your feelings, but you won't let me say the other thing, you know. The palanquin from Lady Lavander's! I should think not. You might as well mistake one of those horrible paper roses that Dorcas sticks in her vases for one of your aunt's Gloires de Dijon! The palanquin from Lady Lavander's—a clumsy human imitation not worth looking at!'

'I didn't know,' said Griselda humbly. 'Do they make such beautiful things in Mandarin Land?'

'Of course,' said the cuckoo.

Griselda sat silent for a minute or two, but very soon she recovered her spirits.

'Will you please tell me where we are going?' she asked again.

'You'll see directly,' said the cuckoo; 'not that I mind telling you. There's to be a grand reception at one of the palaces to-night. I thought you'd like to assist at it. It'll give you some idea of what a palace is like. By the by, can you dance?'

'A little,' replied Griselda.

'Ah, well, I dare say you will manage. I've ordered a court dress for you. It will be all ready when we get there.'

'Thank you,' said Griselda.

In a minute or two the palanquin stopped. The cuckoo got out, and Griselda followed him.

She found that they were at the entrance to a *very* much grander palace than the one in her aunt's saloon. The steps leading up to the door were very wide and shallow, and covered with a gold embroidered carpet, which *looked* as if it would be prickly to her bare feet, but which, on the contrary, when she trod upon it, felt softer than the softest moss. She could see very little besides the carpet, for at each side of the steps stood rows and rows of mandarins, all something like, but a great deal grander than, the pair outside her aunt's cabinet; and as the cuckoo hopped and Griselda walked up the staircase, they all, in turn, row by row, began solemnly to nod. It gave them the look of a field of very high grass, through which anyone passing leaves for the moment a trail, till all the heads bob up again into their places.

'What do they mean?' whispered Griselda.

'It's a royal salute,' said the cuckoo.

'A salute!' said Griselda. 'I thought that meant kissing or guns.'

'Hush!' said the cuckoo, for by this time they had arrived at the top of the staircase; 'you must be dressed now.'

Two mandariny-looking young ladies, with porcelain faces and three-cornered head-dresses, stepped forward and led Griselda into a small ante-room, where lay waiting for her the most magnificent dress you ever saw. But how *do* you think they dressed her? It was all by nodding. They nodded to the blue and silver embroidered jacket, and in a moment it had fitted itself on to her. They nodded to the splendid scarlet satin skirt, made very short in front and very long behind, and before Griselda knew where she was, it was adjusted quite correctly. They nodded to the head-dress, and the sashes, and the necklaces and bracelets, and forthwith they all arranged themselves. Last of all, they nodded to the dearest, sweetest little pair of high-heeled shoes imaginable—all silver, and blue, and gold, and scarlet, and everything mixed up together, *only* they were rather a stumpy shape about the toes, and Griselda's bare feet were encased in them, and, to her surprise, quite comfortably so.

'They don't hurt me a bit,' she said aloud; 'yet they didn't look the least the shape of my foot.'

E

But her attendants only nodded; and turning round, she saw the cuckoo waiting for her. He did not speak either, rather to her annoyance, but gravely led the way through one grand room after another to the grandest of all, where the entertainment was evidently just about to begin. And everywhere there were mandarins, rows and rows, who all set to work nodding as fast as Griselda appeared. She began to be rather tired of royal salutes, and was glad when at last, in profound silence, the procession, consisting of the cuckoo and herself, and about half a dozen 'mandarins,' came to a halt before a kind of dais, or raised seat, at the end of the hall.

Upon this dais stood a chair—a throne of some kind, Griselda supposed it to be—and upon this was seated the grandest and gravest personage she had yet seen.

'Is he king of the mandarins?' she whispered. But the cuckoo did not reply; and before she had time to repeat the question, the very grand and grave person got down from his seat, and coming towards her, offered her his hand, at the same time nodding—first once, then two or three times together, then once again. Griselda seemed to know what he meant. He was asking her to dance.

'Thank you,' she said. 'I can't dance *very* well, but perhaps you won't mind.'

The king, if that was his title, took not the slightest notice of her reply, but nodded again—once, then two or three times together, then once alone, just as before.

But how do you think they dressed her?

Griselda did not know what to do, when suddenly she
felt something poking her head.   It was the cuckoo—
he had lifted his claw, and was tapping her head to
make her nod.   So she nodded—once, twice together
then once—that appeared to be enough.   The king
nodded once again; an invisible band suddenly struck
up the loveliest music, and off they set to the places of
honour reserved for them in the centre of the room,
where all the mandarins were assembling.

What a dance that was!   It began like a minuet and
ended something like the haymakers.   Griselda had
not the least idea what the figures or steps were, but it
did not matter.   If she did not know, her shoes or
something about her did; for she got on famously.
The music was lovely—'so the mandarins can't be
deaf, though they are dumb,' thought Griselda, 'which
is one good thing about them.'   The king seemed to
enjoy it as much as she did, though he never smiled
or laughed; anyone could have seen he liked it
by the way he whirled and twirled himself about.
And between the figures, when they stopped to
rest for a little, Griselda got on very well too.   There
was no conversation, or rather, if there was, it was all
nodding.

So Griselda nodded too, and though she did not
know what her nods meant, the king seemed to understand and be quite pleased; and when they had nodded
enough, the music struck up again, and off they set,
harder than before.

And every now and then tiny little mandariny boys

appeared with trays filled with the most delicious fruits and sweetmeats.   Griselda was not a greedy child, but for once in her life she really *did* feel rather so.   I cannot possibly describe these delicious things; just think of whatever in all your life was the most 'lovely' thing you ever eat, and you may be sure they tasted like that. Only the cuckoo would not eat any, which rather distressed Griselda. He walked about among the dancers, apparently quite at home; and the mandarins did not seem at all surprised to see him, though he did look rather odd, being nearly, if not quite, as big as any of them.   Griselda hoped he was enjoying himself, considering that she had to thank him for all the fun *she* was having, but she felt a little conscience-stricken when she saw that he wouldn't eat anything.

'Cuckoo,' she whispered; she dared not talk out loud —it would have seemed so remarkable, you see. 'Cuckoo,' she said, very, very softly, 'I wish you would eat something.   You'll be so tired and hungry.'

'No, thank you,' said the cuckoo; and you can't think how pleased Griselda was at having succeeded in making him speak.   'It isn't my way.   I hope you are enjoying yourself?'

'Oh, *very* much,' said Griselda.   'I——'

'Hush!' said the cuckoo; and looking up, Griselda saw a number of mandarins, in a sort of procession, coming their way.

When they got up to the cuckoo they set to work nodding, two or three at a time, more energetically than usual.   When they stopped, the cuckoo nodded in

return, and then hopped off towards the middle of the
room.

'They're very fond of good music, you see,' he
whispered as he passed Griselda; 'and they don't often
get it.'

PICTURES

And she is always beautiful,
And always is eighteen!

When he got to the middle of the room the cuckoo cleared his throat, flapped his wings, and began to sing. Griselda was quite astonished. She had had no idea that her friend was so accomplished. It wasn't 'cuckooing' at all; it was real singing, like that of the nightingale or the thrush, or like something prettier than either. It made Griselda think of woods in summer, and of tinkling brooks flowing through them, with the pretty brown pebbles sparkling up through the water; and then it made her think of something sad —she didn't know what; perhaps it was of the babes in the wood and the robins covering them up with leaves—and then again, in a moment, it sounded as if all the merry elves and sprites that ever were heard of had escaped from fairyland, and were rolling over and over with peals of rollicking laughter. And at last, all of a sudden, the song came to an end.

'Cuckoo! cuckoo! cuckoo!' rang out three times, clear and shrill. The cuckoo flapped his wings, made a bow to the mandarins, and retired to his old corner.

There was no buzz of talk, as is usual after a performance has come to a close, but there was a great buzz of nodding, and Griselda, wishing to give the cuckoo as much praise as she could, nodded as hard as any of them. The cuckoo really looked quite shy at receiving so much applause. But in a minute or two the music struck up and the dancing began again—one, two, three: it seemed a sort of mazurka this time, which suited the mandarins very well, as it gave them a chance of nodding to mark the time.

Griselda had once learnt the mazurka, so she got on even better than before—only she would have liked it more if her shoes had had sharper toes; they looked so stumpy when she tried to point them. All the same, it was very good fun, and she was not too well pleased when she suddenly felt the little sharp tap of the cuckoo on her head, and heard him whisper:

'Griselda, it's time to go.'

'Oh dear, why?' she asked. 'I'm not a bit tired. Why need we go yet?'

'Obeying orders,' said the cuckoo; and after that Griselda dared not say another word. It was very nearly as bad as being told she had a great deal to learn.

'Must I say good-bye to the king and all the people?' she inquired; but before the cuckoo had time to answer, she gave a little squeal. 'Oh, cuckoo,' she cried, 'you've trod on my foot.'

'I beg your pardon,' said the cuckoo.

'I must take off my shoe; it does so hurt,' she went on.

'Take it off, then,' said the cuckoo.

Griselda stooped to take off her shoe. 'Are we going home in the pal——?' she began to say; but she never

finished the sentence, for just as she had got her shoe off
she felt the cuckoo throw something round her.   It
was the feather mantle.

And Griselda knew nothing more till she opened her
eyes the next morning, and saw the first early rays of
sunshine peeping in through the chinks of the closed
shutters of her little bedroom.

She rubbed her eyes, and sat up in bed.   Could it
have been a dream?

'What could have made me fall asleep so all of a
sudden?' she thought.   'I wasn't the least sleepy at the
mandarins' ball.   What fun it was!   I believe that
cuckoo made me fall asleep on purpose to make me
fancy it was a dream.   *Was* it a dream?'

She began to feel confused and doubtful, when suddenly she felt something hurting her arm, like a little
lump in the bed.   She felt with her hand to see if she
could smooth it away, and drew out—one of the shoes
belonging to her court dress!   The very one she had
held in her hand at the moment the cuckoo spirited
her home again to bed.

'Ah, Mr Cuckoo!' she exclaimed, 'you meant to
play me a trick, but you haven't succeeded, you see.'

She jumped out of bed and unfastened one of the
window-shutters, then jumped in again to admire the
little shoe in comfort.   It was even prettier than she
had thought it at the ball.   She held it up and looked
at it.   It was about the size of the first joint of her little
finger.   'To think that I should have been dancing
with you on last night!' she said to the shoe.   'And

yet the cuckoo says being big or little is all a matter of fancy. I wonder what he'll think of to amuse me next?'

She was still holding up the shoe and admiring it when Dorcas came with the hot water.

'Look, Dorcas,' she said.

'Bless me, it's one of the shoes off the Chinese dolls in the saloon,' exclaimed the old servant. 'How ever did you get that, missie? Your aunts wouldn't be pleased.'

'It just isn't one of the Chinese dolls' shoes, and if you don't believe me, you can go and look for yourself,' said Griselda. 'It's my very own shoe, and it was given me to my own self.'

Dorcas looked at her curiously, but said no more, only as she was going out of the room Griselda heard her saying something about 'so very like Miss Sybilla.'

'I wonder what "Miss Sybilla" *was* like?' thought Griselda. 'I have a good mind to ask the cuckoo. He seems to have known her very well.'

It was not for some days that Griselda had a chance of asking the cuckoo anything. She saw and heard nothing of him—nothing, that is to say, but his regular appearance to tell the hours as usual.

'I suppose,' thought Griselda, 'he thinks the mandarins' ball was fun enough to last me a good while. It really was very good-natured of him to take me to it, so I mustn't grumble.'

A few days after this poor Griselda caught cold. It was not a very bad cold, I must confess, but her aunts made rather a fuss about it. They wanted her to stay in bed, but to this Griselda so much objected that they did not insist upon it.

'It would be so dull,' she said piteously. 'Please let me stay in the ante-room, for all my things are there; and, then, there's the cuckoo.'

Aunt Grizzel smiled at this, and Griselda got her way. But even in the ante-room it was rather dull. Miss Grizzel and Miss Tabitha were obliged to go out, to drive all the way to Merrybrow Hall, as Lady Lavander sent a messenger to say that she had an attack of influenza, and wished to see her friends at once.

Miss Tabitha began to cry—she was so tender-hearted.

'Troubles never come singly,' said Miss Grizzel, by way of consolation.

'No, indeed, they never come singly,' said Miss Tabitha, shaking her head and wiping her eyes.

So off they set; and Griselda, in her arm-chair by the ante-room fire, with some queer little old-fashioned books of her aunts', which she had already read more than a dozen times, beside her by way of amusement, felt that there was one comfort in her troubles—she had escaped the long weary drive to her godmother's.

But it was very dull. It got duller and duller. Griselda curled herself up in her chair, and wished she could go to sleep, though feeling quite sure she couldn't, for she had stayed in bed much later than usual this morning, and had been obliged to spend the time in sleeping, for want of anything better to do.

She looked up at the clock.

'I don't know even what to wish for,' she said to herself.   'I don't feel the least inclined to play at anything, and I shouldn't care to go to the mandarins again. Oh, cuckoo, cuckoo, I am so dull; couldn't you think of anything to amuse me?'

It was not near 'any o'clock.'   But after waiting a minute or two, it seemed to Griselda that she heard the soft sound of 'coming' that always preceded the cuckoo's appearance.   She was right.   In another moment she heard his usual greeting: 'Cuckoo, cuckoo!'

'Oh, cuckoo!' she exclaimed, 'I am so glad you have come at last.   I *am* so dull, and it has nothing to do with lessons this time.   It's that I've got such a bad cold, and my head's aching, and I'm so tired of reading, all by myself.'

'What would you like to do?' said the cuckoo.   'You don't want to go to see the mandarins again?'

'Oh no; I couldn't dance.'

'Or the mermaids down under the sea?'

'Oh, dear, no,' said Griselda, with a little shiver, 'it would be far too cold.   I would just like to stay where I am, if someone would tell me stories.   I'm not even sure that I could listen to stories.   What could you do to amuse me, cuckoo?'

'Would you like to see some pictures?' said the cuckoo.   'I could show you pictures without your taking any trouble.'

'Oh yes, that would be beautiful,' cried Griselda. 'What pictures will you show me?   Oh, I know.   I

would like to see the place where you were born—
where that very, very clever man made you and the
clock, I mean.'

'Your great-great-grandfather,' said the cuckoo.
'Very well. Now, Griselda, shut your eyes. First of
all, I am going to sing.'

Griselda shut her eyes, and the cuckoo began his
song. It was something like what he had sung at the
mandarins' palace, only even more beautiful. It was
so soft and dreamy, Griselda felt as if she could have
sat there for ever, listening to it.

The first notes were low and murmuring. Again
they made Griselda think of little rippling brooks in
summer, and now and then there came a sort of hum as
of insects buzzing in the warm sunshine near. This
humming gradually increased, till at last Griselda was
conscious of nothing more—*everything* seemed to be
humming, herself too, till at last she fell asleep.

When she opened her eyes, the ante-room and everything in it, except the arm-chair on which she was still
curled up, had disappeared—melted away into a misty
cloud all round her, which in turn gradually faded, till
before her she saw a scene quite new and strange. It
was the first of the cuckoo's 'pictures.'

An old, quaint room, with a high, carved mantelpiece, and a bright fire sparkling in the grate. It was
not a pretty room—it had more the look of a workshop
of some kind; but it was curious and interesting. All
round, the walls were hung with clocks and strange
mechanical toys. There was a fiddler slowly fiddling,

a gentleman and lady gravely dancing a minuet, a little man drawing up water in a bucket out of a glass vase in which goldfish were swimming about—all sorts of queer figures; and the clocks were even queerer. There was one intended to represent the sun, moon, and planets, with one face for the sun and another for the moon and gold and silver stars slowly circling round them; there

He was a very old man . . .

was another clock with a tiny trumpeter perched on a
ledge above the face, who blew a horn for the hours.   I
cannot tell you half the strange and wonderful things
there were.

Griselda was so interested in looking at all these queer
machines, that she did not for some time observe the
occupant of the room.   And no wonder; he was sitting
in front of a little table, so perfectly still, much more
still than the un-living figures around him.   He was
examining, with a magnifying-glass, some small object
he held in his hand, so closely and intently that Griselda,
forgetting she was only looking at a 'picture,' almost
held her breath for fear she should disturb him.   He
was a very old man, his coat was worn and threadbare in
several places, looking as if he spent a great part of his
life in one position.   Yet he did not look *poor*, and his
face, when at last he lifted it, was mild and intelligent
and very earnest.

While Griselda was watching him closely there came
a soft tap at the door, and a little girl danced into the

room. The dearest little girl you ever saw, and *so* funnily dressed! Her thick brown hair, rather lighter than Griselda's, was tied in two long plaits down her back. She had a short red skirt with silver braid round the bottom, and a white chemisette with beautiful lace at the throat and wrists and over that again a black velvet bodice, also trimmed with silver. And she had a great many trinkets, necklaces and bracelets and earrings, and a sort of little silver coronet; no, it was not like a coronet, it was a band with a square piece of silver fastened so as to stand up at each side of her head something like a horse's blinkers, only they were not placed over her eyes.

She made quite a jingle as she came into the room, and the old man looked up with a smile of pleasure.

'Well, my darling, and are you all ready for your fête?' he said; and though the language in which he spoke was quite strange to Griselda, she understood his meaning perfectly well.

'Yes, dear grandfather; and isn't my dress lovely?' said the child. 'I should be *so* happy if only you were coming too, and would get yourself a beautiful velvet coat like Mynheer van Huyten.'

The old man shook his head.

'I have no time for such things, my darling,' he replied; 'and besides, I am too old. I must work—work hard to make money for my pet when I am gone, that she may not be dependent on the bounty of those English sisters.'

'But I won't care for money when you are gone,

grandfather,' said the child, her eyes filling with tears.
'I would rather just go on living in this little house, and
I am sure the neighbours would give me something to
eat, and then I could hear all your clocks ticking, and
think of you. I don't want you to sell all your wonderful things for money for me, grandfather. They would
remind me of you, and money wouldn't.'

'Not all, Sybilla, not all,' said the old man. 'The
best of all, the *chef-d'œuvre* of my life, shall not be
sold. It shall be yours, and you will have in your
possession a clock that crowned heads might seek in
vain to purchase.'

His dim old eyes brightened, and for a moment he
sat erect and strong.

'Do you mean the cuckoo clock?' said Sybilla in a
low voice.

'Yes, my darling, the cuckoo clock, the crowning
work of my life—a clock that shall last long after I, and
perhaps thou, my pretty child, are crumbling into dust;
a clock that shall last to tell my great-grandchildren to
many generations that the old Dutch mechanic was not
altogether to be despised.'

Sybilla sprang into his arms.

'You are not to talk like that, little grandfather,' she
said. 'I shall teach my children and my grandchildren
to be so proud of you—oh, so proud!—as proud as I am
of you, little grandfather.'

'Gently, my darling,' said the old man, as he placed
carefully on the table the delicate piece of mechanism
he held in his hand, and tenderly embraced the child.

F

'Kiss me once again, my pet, and then thou must go; thy little friends will be waiting.'

     •   •   •   •   •

As he said these words the mist slowly gathered again before Griselda's eyes—the first of the cuckoo's pictures faded from her sight.

     •   •   •   •   .

When she looked again the scene was changed but this time it was not a strange one, though Griselda had gazed at it for some moments before she recognized it. It was the great saloon, but it looked very different from what she had ever seen it.   Forty years or so make a difference in rooms as well as in people!

The faded yellow damask hangings were rich and brilliant.   There were bouquets of lovely flowers arranged about the tables; wax lights were sending out their brightness in every direction, and the room was filled with ladies and gentlemen in gay attire.

Among them, after a time, Griselda remarked two ladies, no longer very young, but still handsome and stately, and something whispered to her that they were her two aunts, Miss Grizzel and Miss Tabitha.

'Poor aunts!' she said softly to herself; 'how old they have grown since then.'

But she did not long look at them; her attention was attracted by a much younger lady—a mere girl she seemed, but oh, so sweet and pretty!   She was dancing with a gentleman whose eyes looked as if they saw no one else, and she herself seemed brimming over with youth and happiness. Her very steps had joy in them.

'Well, Griselda,' whispered a voice, which she knew was the cuckoo's, 'so you don't like to be told you are like your grandmother, eh?'

Griselda turned round sharply to look for the speaker, but he was not to be seen. And when she turned again the picture of the great saloon had faded away.

.   .   .   .   .

One more picture.

Griselda looked again. She saw before her a country road in full summer time; the sun was shining, the birds were singing, the trees covered with their bright green leaves—everything appeared happy and joyful. But at last in the distance she saw, slowly approaching, a group of a few people, all walking together, carrying in their centre something long and narrow, which, though the black cloth covering it was almost hidden by the white flowers with which it was thickly strewn, Griselda knew to be a coffin.

It was a funeral procession, and in the place of chief mourner, with pale, set face, walked the same young man whom Griselda had last seen dancing with the girl Sybilla in the great saloon.

The sad group passed slowly out of sight; but as it disappeared there fell upon the ear the sounds of sweet music, lovelier far than she had heard before—lovelier than the magic cuckoo's most lovely songs — and somehow, in the music, it seemed to the child's fancy there were mingled the soft strains of a woman's voice.

'It is Sybilla singing,' thought Griselda dreamily, and with that she fell asleep again.

.   .   .   .   .

When she woke she was in the arm-chair by the ante-room fire, everything around her looking just as usual, the cuckoo clock ticking away calmly and regularly. Had it been a dream only? Griselda could not make up her mind.

'But I don't see that it matters if it was,' she said to herself. 'If it was a dream, the cuckoo sent it to me all the same, and I thank you very much indeed, cuckoo,' she went on, looking up at the clock. 'The last picture was rather sad, but still it was very nice to see it, and I thank you very much, and I'll never say again that I don't like to be told I'm like my dear pretty grandmother.'

The cuckoo took no notice of what she said, but Griselda did not mind. She was getting used to his 'ways.'

'I expect he hears me quite well,' she thought; 'and even if he doesn't, it's only civil to *try* to thank him.'

She sat still contentedly enough, thinking over what she had seen, and trying to make more 'pictures' for herself in the fire. Then there came faintly to her ears the sound of carriage wheels, opening and shutting of doors, a little bustle of arrival.

'My aunts must have come back,' thought Griselda;

and so it was. In a few minutes Miss Grizzel, closely followed by Miss Tabitha, appeared at the ante-room door.

'Well, my love,' said Miss Grizzel anxiously, 'and how are you? Has the time seemed very long while we were away?'

'Oh no, thank you, Aunt Grizzel,' replied Griselda, not at all. I've been quite happy, and my cold's ever so much better, and my headache's *quite* gone.'

'Come, that is good news,' said Miss Grizzel. 'Not that I'm exactly *surprised*,' she continued, turning to Miss Tabitha, 'for there really is nothing like tansy tea for a feverish cold.'

'Nothing,' agreed Miss Tabitha, 'there really is nothing like it.'

'Aunt Grizzel,' said Griselda, after a few moments' silence, 'was my grandmother quite young when she died?'

'Yes, my love, very young,' replied Miss Grizzel with a change in her voice.

'And was her husband *very* sorry?' pursued Griselda.

'Heart-broken,' said Miss Grizzel. 'He did not live long after, and then you know, my dear, your father was sent to us to take care of. And now he has sent *you*—the third generation of young creatures confided to our care.'

'Yes,' said Griselda. 'My grandmother died in the summer, when all the flowers were out; and she was buried in a pretty country place, wasn't she?'

'Yes,' said Miss Grizzel, looking rather bewildered.

'And when she was a little girl she lived with her grandfather, the old Dutch mechanic,' continued Griselda, unconsciously using the very words she had heard in her vision. 'He was a nice old man; and how clever of him to have made the cuckoo clock, and such lots of other pretty, wonderful things. I don't wonder little Sybilla loved him; he was so good to her. But, oh, Aunt Grizzel, *how* pretty she was when she was a young lady! That time that she danced with my grandfather in the great saloon. And how very nice you and Aunt Tabitha looked then, too.'

Miss Grizzel held her very breath in astonishment; and no doubt if Miss Tabitha had known she was doing so, she would have held hers too. But Griselda lay still, gazing at the fire, quite unconscious of her aunt's surprise.

'Your papa told you all these old stories, I suppose, my dear,' said Miss Grizzel at last.

'Oh no,' said Griselda dreamily. 'Papa never told me anything like that. Dorcas told me a very little, I think; at least, she made me want to know, and I asked the cuckoo, and then, you see, he showed me it all. It was so pretty.'

Miss Grizzel glanced at her sister.

'Tabitha, my dear,' she said in a low voice, 'do you hear?'

And Miss Tabitha, who really was not very deaf when she set herself to hear, nodded in awestruck silence.

'Tabitha,' continued Miss Grizzel in the same tone,

'. . . there really is nothing like tansy tea for a feverish cold'

'it is wonderful! Ah, yes, how true it is, Tabitha, that "there are more things in heaven and earth than are dreamt of in our philosophy"' (for Miss Grizzel was a well-read old lady, you see); 'and from the very first, Tabitha, we always had a feeling that the child was strangely like Sybilla.'

'Strangely like Sybilla,' echoed Miss Tabitha.

'May she grow up as good, if not quite as beautiful —*that* we could scarcely expect; and may she be longer spared to those that love her,' added Miss Grizzel, bending over Griselda, while two or three tears slowly trickled down her aged cheeks. 'See, Tabitha, the dear child is fast asleep. How sweet she looks! I trust by to-morrow morning she will be quite herself again: her cold is so much better.

VI

Rubbed the Wrong Way

*For now and then there comes a day
When everything goes wrong.*

GRISELDA'S cold *was* much better by 'to-morrow morning.' In fact, I might almost say it was quite well.

But Griselda herself did not feel quite well, and saying this reminds me that it is hardly sense to speak of a *cold* being better or well—for a cold's being 'well' means that it is not there at all, out of existence, in short, and if a thing is out of existence how can we say anything about it? Children, I feel quite in a hobble —I cannot get my mind straight about it—please think it over and give me your opinion. In the meantime, I will go on about Griselda.

She felt just a little ill—a sort of feeling that sometimes is rather nice, sometimes 'very extremely' much the reverse! She felt in the humour for being petted, and having beef-tea, and jelly, and sponge cake with her tea, and for a day or two this was all very well. She *was* petted, and she had lots of beef-tea, and jelly, and grapes, and sponge cakes, and everything nice, for her aunts, as you must have seen by this time, were really very, very kind to her in every way in which they understood how to be so.

79

But after a few days of the continued petting, and the beef-tea and the jelly and all the rest of it, it occurred to Miss Grizzel, who had a good large bump of 'common sense,' that it might be possible to overdo this sort of thing.

'Tabitha,' she said to her sister, when they were sitting together in the evening after Griselda had gone to bed, 'Tabitha, my dear, I think the child is quite well again now. It seems to me it would be well to send a note to good Mr Kneebreeches, to say that she will be able to resume her studies the day after to-morrow.'

'The day after to-morrow,' repeated Miss Tabitha. 'The day after to-morrow—to say that she will be able to resume her studies the day after to-morrow—oh yes, certainly. It would be very well to send a note to good Mr Kneebreeches, my dear Grizzel.'

'I thought you would agree with me,' said Miss Grizzel, with a sigh of relief (as if poor Miss Tabitha during all the last half-century had ever ventured to do anything else), getting up to fetch her writing materials as she spoke. 'It is such a satisfaction to consult together about what we do. I was only a little afraid of being hard upon the child, but as you agree with me, I have no longer any misgiving.'

'Any misgiving, oh dear, no!' said Miss Tabitha. 'You have no reason for any misgiving, I am sure, my dear Grizzel.'

So the note was written and dispatched, and the next morning when, about twelve o'clock, Griselda made her appearance in the little drawing-room where her aunts usually sat, looking, it must be confessed, very plump and rosy for an invalid, Miss Grizzel broached the subject.

'I have written to request Mr Kneebreeches to resume his instructions to-morrow,' she said quietly. 'I think you are quite well again now, so Dorcas must wake you at your usual hour.'

Griselda had been settling herself comfortably on a corner of the sofa. She had got a nice book to read, which her father, hearing of her illness, had sent her by post, and she was looking forward to the tempting plateful of jelly which Dorcas had brought her for luncheon every day since she had been ill. Altogether, she was feeling very 'lazy-easy' and contented. Her aunt's announcement felt like a sudden downpour of cold water, or rush of east wind. She sat straight up on her sofa, and exclaimed in a tone of great annoyance:

'*Oh*, Aunt Grizzel!'

'Well, my dear?' said Miss Grizzel placidly.

'I *wish* you wouldn't make me begin lessons again just yet. I *know* they'll make my head ache again, and Mr Kneebreeches will be *so* cross. I know he will, and he is so horrid when he is cross.'

'Hush!' said Miss Grizzel, holding up her hand in a way that reminded Griselda of the cuckoo's favourite 'obeying orders.' Just then, too, in the distance the ante-room clock struck twelve. 'Cuckoo! cuckoo! cuckoo!' on it went. Griselda could have stamped with irritation, but *somehow*, in spite of herself, she felt compelled to say nothing. She muttered some not very pretty words, coiled herself round on the sofa, opened her book, and began to read.

But it was not as interesting as she had expected. She had not read many pages before she began to yawn, and she was delighted to be interrupted by Dorcas and the jelly.

But the jelly was not as nice as she had expected, either. She tasted it, and thought it was too sweet; and when she tasted it again, it seemed too strong of cinnamon; and the third taste seemed too strong of everything. She laid down her spoon and looked about her discontentedly.

'What is the matter, my dear?' said Miss Grizzel. 'Is the jelly not to your liking?'

'I don't know,' said Griselda shortly. She ate a few spoonfuls, and then took up her book again. Miss Grizzel said nothing more, but to herself she thought that Mr Kneebreeches had not been recalled any too soon.

All day long it was much the same. Nothing seemed to come right to Griselda. It was a dull, cold day, what is called 'a black frost'; not a bright, clear, *pretty*, cold day, but the sort of frost that really makes the world seem dead—makes it almost impossible to believe that there will ever be warmth and sound and 'growing-ness' again.

Late in the afternoon Griselda crept up to the ante-room, and sat down by the window. Outside it was nearly dark, and inside it was not much more cheerful

—for the fire was nearly out, and no lamps were lighted; only the cuckoo clock went on tick-ticking briskly as usual.

'I hate winter,' said Griselda, pressing her cold little face against the colder window-pane, 'I hate winter, and I hate lessons. I would give up being a *person* in a minute if I might be a—a—what would I best like to be? Oh yes, I know—a butterfly. Butterflies never see winter, and they *certainly* never have any lessons or any kind of work to do. I hate *must*-ing to do anything.'

'Cuckoo,' rang out suddenly above her head.

It was only four o'clock striking, and as soon as he had told it the cuckoo was back behind his doors again in an instant, just as usual. There was nothing for Griselda to feel offended at, but somehow she got quite angry.

'I don't care what you think, cuckoo!' she exclaimed defiantly. 'I know you came out on purpose just now, but I don't care. I *do* hate winter, and I *do* hate lessons, and I *do* think it would be nicer to be a butterfly than a little girl.'

In her secret heart I fancy she was half in hopes that the cuckoo would come out again, and talk things over with her. Even if he were to scold her, she felt that it would be better than sitting there alone with nobody to speak to, which was very dull work indeed. At the bottom of her conscience there lurked the knowledge that what she *should* be doing was to be looking over her last lessons with Mr Kneebreeches, and refreshing her memory for the next day; but, alas! knowing one's duty is by no means the same thing as doing it, and Griselda sat on by the window doing nothing but grumble and work herself up into a belief that she was one of the most-to-be-pitied little girls in all the world. So that by the time Dorcas came to call her to tea I doubt if she had a single pleasant thought or feeling left in her heart.

Things grew no better after tea, and before long Griselda asked if she might go to bed. She was 'so tired,' she said; and she certainly looked so, for ill humour and idleness are excellent 'tirers,' and will soon take the roses out of a child's cheeks and the brightness out of her eyes. She held up her face to be kissed by her aunts in a meekly reproachful way, which made the old ladies feel quite uncomfortable.

'I am by no means sure that I have done right in recalling Mr Kneebreeches so soon, Sister Tabitha,' remarked Miss Grizzel uneasily, when Griselda had left the room. But Miss Tabitha was busy counting her stitches, and did not give full attention to Miss Grizzel's observation, so she just repeated placidly: 'Oh yes, Sister Grizzel, you may be sure you have done right in recalling Mr Kneebreeches.'

'I am glad you think so,' said Miss Grizzel, with again a little sigh of relief. 'I was only distressed to see the child looking so white and tired.'

Upstairs Griselda was hurry-scurrying into bed. There was a lovely fire in her room—fancy that! Was she not a poor neglected little creature? But even this

did not please her. She was too cross to be pleased
with anything; too cross to wash her face and hands, or
let Dorcas brush her hair out nicely as usual; too cross,
alas, to say her prayers! She just huddled into bed,
huddling up her mind in an untidy hurry and con-
fusion, just as she left her clothes in an untidy heap on
the floor. She would not look into herself, was the
truth of it; she shrank from doing so because she *knew*
things had been going on in that silly little heart of
hers in a most unsatisfactory way all day, and she wanted
to go to sleep and forget all about it.

She did go to sleep, very quickly too. No doubt she
really was tired; tired with crossness and doing nothing,
and she slept very soundly. When she woke up she
felt so refreshed and rested that she fancied it must be
morning. It was dark, of course, but that was to be
expected in mid winter, especially as the shutters were
closed.

'I wonder,' thought Griselda, 'I wonder if it really *is*
morning. I should like to get up early—I went so
early to bed. I think I'll just jump out of bed and
open a chink of the shutters. I'll see at once if it's
nearly morning by the look of the sky.'

She was up in a minute, feeling her way across the
room to the window, and without much difficulty she
found the hook of the shutters, unfastened it, and threw
one side open. Ah no, there was no sign of morning
to be seen. There was moonlight, but nothing else,
and not so very much of that, for the clouds were hurrying across the 'orbèd maiden's' face at such a rate, one

after the other, that the light was more like a number of pale flashes than the steady, cold shining of most frosty moonlight nights. There was going to be a change of weather, and the cloud armies were collecting together from all quarters; that was the real explanation of the hurrying and scurrying Griselda saw overhead, but this, of course, she did not understand. She only saw that it looked wild and stormy, and she shivered a little, partly with cold, partly with a half-frightened feeling that she could not have explained.

'I had better go back to bed,' she said to herself; 'but I am not a bit sleepy.'

She was just drawing-to the shutter again when something caught her eye, and she stopped short in surprise. A little bird was outside on the window-sill —a tiny bird crouching in close to the cold glass. Griselda's kind heart was touched in an instant. Cold as she was, she pushed back the shutter again, and drawing a chair forward to the window, managed to unfasten it—it was not a very heavy one—and to open it wide enough to slip her hand gently along to the bird. It did not start or move.

'Can it be dead?' thought Griselda anxiously.

But no, it was not dead. It let her put her hand round it and draw it in, and to her delight she felt that it was soft and warm, and it even gave a gentle peck on her thumb.

'Poor little bird, how cold you must be,' she said kindly. But, to her amazement, no sooner was the bird safely inside the room, than it managed cleverly to escape from her hand. It fluttered quietly up on to her shoulder, and sang out in a soft but cheery tone: 'Cuckoo, cuckoo —cold, did you say, Griselda? Not so very, thank you.'

Griselda stepped back from the window.

'It's *you*, is it?' she said rather surlily, her tone seeming to infer that she had taken a great deal of trouble for nothing.

'Of course it is, and why shouldn't it be? You're not generally so sorry to see me. What's the matter?'

'Nothing's the mat-ter,' replied Griselda,

'*Poor little bird, how cold you must be*'

feeling a little ashamed of her want of civility; 'only, you see, if I had known it was *you*——' She hesitated.

'You wouldn't have clambered up and hurt your poor fingers in opening the window if you had known it was me—is that it, eh?' said the cuckoo.

Somehow, when the cuckoo said 'eh?' like that, Griselda was obliged to tell just what she was thinking.

'No, I wouldn't have *needed* to open the window,' she

G

said. '*You* can get in or out whenever you like; you're not like a real bird. Of course, you were just tricking me, sitting out there and pretending to be a starved robin.'

There was a little indignation in her voice, and she gave her head a toss which nearly upset the cuckoo.

'Dear me, dear me!' exclaimed the cuckoo. 'You have a great deal to complain of, Griselda. Your time and strength must be very valuable for you to regret so much having wasted a little of them on me.'

Griselda felt her face grow red. What did he mean? Did he know how yesterday had been spent? She said nothing, but she drooped her head, and one or two tears came slowly creeping up to her eyes.

'Child!' said the cuckoo, suddenly changing his tone, 'you are very foolish. Is a kind thought or action *ever* wasted? Can your eyes see what such good seeds grow into? They have wings, Griselda —kindnesses have wings and roots, remember that —wings that never droop and roots that never die. What do you think I came and sat outside your window for?'

'Cuckoo,' said Griselda humbly, 'I am very sorry.'

'Very well,' said the cuckoo, 'we'll leave it for the present. I have something else to see about. Are you cold, Griselda?'

'*Very*,' she replied. 'I would very much like to go back to bed, cuckoo, if you please; and there's plenty of room for you too, if you'd like to come in and get warm.'

'There are other ways of getting warm besides going to bed,' said the cuckoo. 'A nice brisk walk, for instance. I was going to ask you to come out into the garden with me.'

Griselda almost screamed.

'Out into the garden! *Oh*, cuckoo!' she exclaimed, 'how can you think of such a thing? Such a freezing cold night. Oh no, indeed, cuckoo, I couldn't possibly.'

'Very well, Griselda,' said the cuckoo; 'if you haven't yet learnt to trust me there's no more to be said. Good night.'

He flapped his wings, cried out 'Cuckoo' once only, flew across the room, and almost before Griselda understood what he was doing, had disappeared.

She hurried after him, stumbling against the furniture in her haste, and by the uncertain light. The door was not open, but the cuckoo had got through it—'by the keyhole, I dare say,' thought Griselda; 'he can "scrooge" himself up any way'—for a faint 'Cuckoo' was to be heard on its other side. In a moment Griselda had opened it, and was speeding down the long passage in the dark, guided only by the voice from time to time heard before her: 'Cuckoo, cuckoo.'

She forgot all about the cold, or rather, she did not feel it, though the floor was of uncarpeted old oak, whose hard, polished surface would have usually felt like ice to a child's soft, bare feet. It was a very long passage, and to-night, somehow, it seemed longer than ever. In fact, Griselda could have fancied she had been running along it for half a mile or more, when at last she was brought to a standstill by finding she could go no further. Where was she? She could not imagine! It must be a part of the house she had never explored in the daytime, she decided. In front of her was a little stair running downwards, and ending in a doorway. All this Griselda could see by a bright light that streamed in by the keyhole and through the chinks round the door—a light so brilliant that the little girl blinked her eyes, and for a moment felt quite dazzled and confused.

'It came so suddenly,' she said to herself; 'someone must have lighted a lamp in there all at once. But it can't be a lamp, it's too bright for a lamp. It's more like the sun; but however could the sun be shining in a room in the middle of the night? What shall I do? Shall I open the door and peep in?'

'Cuckoo, cuckoo,' came the answer, soft but clear, from the other side.

'Can it be a trick of the cuckoo's to get me out into the garden?' thought Griselda; and for the first time since she had run out of her room a shiver of cold made her teeth chatter and her skin feel creepy.

'Cuckoo, cuckoo,' sounded again, nearer this time, it seemed to Griselda.

'He's waiting for me. I *will* trust him,' she said resolutely. 'He has always been good and kind, and it's horrid of me to think he's going to trick me.'

She ran down the little stair, she seized the handle of the door. It turned easily; the door opened—

opened, and closed again noiselessly behind her, and what do you think she saw?

'Shut your eyes for a minute, Griselda,' said the cuckoo's voice beside her; 'the light will dazzle you at first. Shut them, and I will brush them with a little daisy dew, to strengthen them.'

Griselda did as she was told. She felt the tip of the cuckoo's softest feather pass gently two or three times over her eyelids, and a delicious scent seemed immediately to float before her.

'I didn't know *daisies* had any scent,' she remarked.

'Perhaps you didn't. You forget, Griselda, that you have a great——'

'Oh, please don't, cuckoo. Please, please don't, *dear* cuckoo,' she exclaimed, dancing about with her hands clasped in entreaty, but her eyes still firmly closed. 'Don't say that, and I'll promise to believe whatever you tell me. And how soon may I open my eyes, please, cuckoo?'

'Turn round slowly, three times. That will give the dew time to take effect,' said the cuckoo. 'Here goes—one—two—three. There, now.'

Griselda opened her eyes.

VII

Butterfly Land

I'd be a butterfly

Griselda opened her eyes.

What did she see?

The loveliest, loveliest garden that ever or never a little girl's eyes saw. As for describing it, I cannot. I must leave a good deal to your fancy. It was just a *delicious* garden. There was a charming mixture of all that is needed to make a garden perfect—grass, velvety lawn rather; water, for a little brook ran tinkling in and out, playing bo-peep among the bushes; trees, of course, and flowers, of course, flowers of every shade and shape. But all these beautiful things Griselda did not at first give as much attention to as they deserved; her eyes were so occupied with a quite unusual sight that met them.

This was butterflies! Not that butterflies are so very uncommon; but butterflies, as Griselda saw them, I am quite sure, children, none of you ever saw, or are likely to see. There were such enormous numbers of them, and the variety of their colours and sizes was so great. They were fluttering about everywhere; the garden seemed actually alive with them.

Griselda stood for a moment in silent delight, feasting

her eyes on the lovely things before her, enjoying the delicious sunshine which kissed her poor little bare feet and seemed to wrap her all up in its warm embrace. Then she turned to her little friend.

'Cuckoo,' she said, 'I thank you *so* much. This *is* fairyland, at last!'

The cuckoo smiled, I was going to say, but that would be a figure of speech only, would it not? He shook his head gently.

'No, Griselda,' he said kindly, 'this is only Butterfly Land.'

'*Butterfly* Land!' repeated Griselda, with a little disappointment in her tone.

'Well,' said the cuckoo, 'it's where you were wishing to be yesterday, isn't it?'

Griselda did not particularly like these allusions to 'yesterday.' She thought it would be as well to change the subject.

'It's a beautiful place, whatever it is,' she said, 'and I'm sure, cuckoo, I'm *very* much obliged to you for bringing me here. Now may I run about and look at everything? How delicious it is to feel the warm sunshine again! I didn't know how cold I was. Look, cuckoo, my toes and fingers are quite blue; they're only just beginning to come right again. I suppose the sun always shines here. How nice it must be to be a butterfly; don't you think so, cuckoo? Nothing to do but fly about.'

She stopped at last, quite out of breath.

'Griselda,' said the cuckoo, 'if you want me to answer

your questions, you must ask them one at a time. You
may run about and look at everything if you like, but
you had better not be in such a hurry. You will make
a great many mistakes if you are—you have made some
already.'

'How?' said Griselda.

'*Have* the butterflies nothing to do but fly about?
Watch them.'

Griselda watched.

'They do seem to be doing something,' she said, at
last, 'but I can't think what. They seem to be nibbling
at the flowers and then flying away, something like
bees gathering honey. *Butterflies* don't gather honey,
cuckoo?'

'No,' said the cuckoo. 'They are filling their paint-
boxes.'

'What *do* you mean?' said Griselda.

'Come and see,' said the cuckoo.

He flew quietly along in front of her, leading the
way through the prettiest paths in all the pretty garden.
The paths were arranged in different colours, as it were;
that is to say, the flowers growing along their sides were
not all 'mixty-maxty,' but one shade after another in
regular order—from the palest blush pink to the very
deepest damask crimson; then, again, from the soft
greenish blue of the small grass forget-me-not to the
rich warm tinge of the brilliant cornflower. *Every*
tint was there; shades to which, though not exactly
strange to her, Griselda could yet have given no name,
for the daisy dew, you see, had sharpened her eyes to

observe delicate variations of colour as she had never
done before.

'How beautifully the flowers are planned,' she said
to the cuckoo.   'Is it just to look pretty, or why?'

'It saves time,' replied the cuckoo.   'The fetch-and-
carry butterflies know exactly where to go to for the
tint the world-flower-painters want.'

'Who are the fetch-and-carry butterflies, and who
are the world-flower-painters?' asked Griselda.

'Wait a bit and you'll see, and use your eyes,'
answered the cuckoo.   'It'll do your tongue no harm
to have a rest now and then.'

Griselda thought it as well to take his advice, though
not particularly relishing the manner in which it was
given.   She did use her eyes, and as she and the cuckoo
made their way along the flower alleys, she saw that
the butterflies were never idle.   They came regularly,
in little parties of twos and threes, and nibbled away, as
she called it, at flowers of the same colour but different
shades, till they had got what they wanted.   Then off
flew butterfly No. 1 with perhaps the palest tint of
maize, or yellow, or lavender, whichever he was in
quest of, followed by No. 2 with the next deeper shade
of the same, and No. 3 bringing up the rear.

Griselda gave a little sigh.

'What's the matter?' said the cuckoo.

'They work very hard,' she replied in a melancholy
tone.

'It's a busy time of year,' observed the cuckoo
dryly.

After a time they came to what seemed to be a sort of centre to the garden. It was a huge glass house, with numberless doors, in and out of which butterflies were incessantly flying—reminding Griselda again of bees and a beehive. But she made no remark till the cuckoo spoke again.

'Come in,' he said.

Griselda had to stoop a good deal, but she did manage to get in without knocking her head or doing any damage. Inside was just a mass of butterflies. A confused mass it seemed at first, but after a while she saw that it was the very reverse of confused. The butterflies were all settled in rows on long, narrow, white tables, and before each was a tiny object about the size of a flattened-out pin's head, which he was most carefully painting with one of his tentacles, which, from time to time, he moistened by rubbing it on the head of a butterfly waiting patiently behind him. Behind this butterfly again stood another, who after a while took his place, while the first attendant flew away.

'To fill his paint-box again,' remarked the cuckoo, who seemed to read Griselda's thoughts.

'But what *are* they painting, cuckoo?' she inquired eagerly.

'All the flowers in the world,' replied the cuckoo. 'Autumn, winter, and spring, they're hard at work. It's only just for the three months of summer that the butterflies have any holiday, and then a few stray ones now and then wander up to the world, and people talk about "idle butterflies"! And even then it isn't true

that they are idle.   They go up to take a look at the
flowers, to see how their work has turned out, and many
a damaged petal they repair, or touch up a faded tint,
though no one ever knows it.'

'*I* know it now,' said Griselda.   'I will never talk
about idle butterflies again—never.   But, cuckoo, do
they paint all the flowers *here*, too?   What a *fearful* lot
they must have to do!'

'No,' said the cuckoo; 'the flowers down here are
fairy flowers.   They never fade or die, they are always
just as you see them.   But the colours of your flowers
are all taken from them, as you have seen.   Of course
they don't look the same up there,' he went on, with
a slight contemptuous shrug of his cuckoo shoulders;
'the coarse air and the ugly things about must take the
bloom off.   The wild flowers do the best, to my thinking; people don't meddle with them in their stupid,
clumsy way.'

'But how do they get the flowers sent up to the world,
cuckoo?' asked Griselda.

'They're packed up, of course, and taken up at night
when all of you are asleep,' said the cuckoo.   'They're
painted on elastic stuff, you see, which fits itself as the
plant grows.   Why, if your eyes were as they are
usually, Griselda, you couldn't even *see* the petals the
butterflies are painting now.'

'And the packing up,' said Griselda; 'do the butterflies do that too?'

'No,' said the cuckoo, 'the fairies look after that.'

'How wonderful!' exclaimed Griselda.   But before

the cuckoo had time to say more a sudden tumult filled the air. It was butterfly dinner-time!

'Are you hungry, Griselda?' said the cuckoo.

'Not so very,' replied Griselda.

'It's just as well perhaps that you're not,' he remarked, 'for I don't know that you'd be much the better for dinner here.'

'Why not?' inquired Griselda curiously. 'What do they have for dinner? Honey? I like that very well, spread on the top of bread-and-butter, of course—I don't think I should care to eat it alone.'

'You won't get any honey,' the cuckoo was beginning; but he was interrupted. Two handsome butterflies flew into the great glass hall, and making straight for the cuckoo, alighted on his shoulders. They fluttered about him for a minute or two, evidently rather excited about something, then flew away again, as suddenly as they had appeared.

'Those were royal messengers,' said the cuckoo, turning to Griselda. 'They have come with a message from the king and queen to invite us to a banquet which is to be held in honour of your visit.'

'What fun!' cried Griselda. 'Do let's go at once, cuckoo. But, oh dear me,' she went on, with a melancholy change of tone, 'I was forgetting, cuckoo. I can't go to the banquet. I have nothing on but my night-gown. I never thought of it before, for I'm not a bit cold.'

'Never mind,' said the cuckoo, 'I'll soon have that put to rights.'

He flew off, and was back almost immediately, followed by a whole flock of butterflies. They were of a smaller kind than Griselda had hitherto seen, and they were of two colours only; half were blue, half yellow. They flew up to Griselda, who felt for a moment as if she were really going to be suffocated by them, but only for a moment. There seemed a great buzz and flutter about her, and then the butterflies set to work to *dress* her. And how do you think they dressed her? With *themselves*! They arranged themselves all over her in the cleverest way. One set of blue ones clustered round the hem of her little white night-gown, making a thick *ruche*, as it were; and then there came two or three thinner rows of yellow, and then blue again. Round her waist they made the loveliest belt of mingled blue and yellow, and all over the upper part of her night-gown, in and out among the pretty white frills which Dorcas herself 'goffered,' so nicely, they made themselves into fantastic trimmings of every shape and kind; bows, rosettes—I cannot tell you what they did not imitate.

Perhaps the prettiest ornament of all was the coronet or wreath they made of themselves for her head, dotting over her curly brown hair too with butterfly spangles, which quivered like dew-drops as she moved about. No one would have known Griselda; she looked like a fairy queen, or princess, at least, for even her little white feet had what *looked* like butterfly shoes upon them, though these, you will understand, were only a sort of make-believe, as, of course, the shoes were soleless.

'Now,' said the cuckoo, when at last all was quiet again, and every blue and every yellow butterfly seemed settled in his place, 'now, Griselda, come and look at yourself.'

He led the way to a marble basin, into which fell the waters of one of the tinkling brooks that were to be found everywhere about the garden, and bade Griselda look into the water mirror. It danced about rather; but still she was quite able to see herself. She peered in with great satisfaction, turning herself round so as to see first over one shoulder, then over the other.

'It *is* lovely,' she said at last. 'But, cuckoo, I'm just thinking—how shall I possibly be able to sit down without crushing ever so many?'

'Bless you, you needn't trouble about that,' said the cuckoo; 'the butterflies are quite able to take care of themselves. You don't suppose you are the first little girl they have ever made a dress for?'

Griselda said no more, but followed the cuckoo, walking rather 'gingerly,' notwithstanding his assurances that the butterflies could take care of themselves. At last the cuckoo stopped in front of a sort of banked-up terrace, in the centre of which grew a strange-looking plant with large, smooth, spreading-out leaves, and on the two topmost leaves, their splendid wings glittering in the sunshine, sat two magnificent butterflies. They were many times larger than any Griselda had yet seen; in fact, the cuckoo himself looked rather small beside them, and they were *so* beautiful that Griselda felt quite overawed. You could not have said what colour they were, for at the faintest movement they seemed to change into new colours, each more exquisite than the last. Perhaps I could best give you an idea of them by saying that they were like living rainbows.

'Are those the king and queen?' asked Griselda in a whisper.

'Yes,' said the cuckoo. 'Do you admire them?'

'I should rather think I did,' said Griselda. 'But, cuckoo, do they never do anything but lie there in the sunshine?'

'Oh, you silly girl,' exclaimed the cuckoo, 'always jumping at conclusions. No, indeed, that is not how they manage things in Butterfly Land. The king and queen have worked harder than any other butterflies. They are chosen every now and then, out of all the others, as being the most industrious and the cleverest of all the world-flower-painters, and then they are allowed to rest, and are fed on the finest essences, so that they grow as splendid as you see. But even now they are not idle; they superintend all the work that is done, and choose all the new colours.'

'Dear me!' said Griselda, under her breath, 'how clever they must be.'

Just then the butterfly king and queen stretched out their magnificent wings, and rose upwards, soaring proudly into the air.

'Are they going away?' said Griselda in a disappointed tone.

'Oh no,' said the cuckoo; 'they are welcoming you. Hold out your hands.'

Griselda held out her hands, and stood gazing up into the sky. In a minute or two the royal butterflies appeared again, slowly, majestically circling downwards, till at length they alighted on Griselda's little hands, the king on the right, the queen on the left, almost covering her fingers with their great dazzling wings.

'You *do* look nice now,' said the cuckoo, hopping back a few steps and looking up at Griselda approvingly; 'but it's time for the feast to begin, as it won't do for us to be late.'

The king and queen appeared to understand. They floated away from Griselda's hands and settled themselves, this time, at one end of a beautiful little grass plot or lawn, just below the terrace where grew the large-leaved plant. This was evidently their dining-room, for no sooner were they in their place than butterflies of every kind and colour came pouring in, in masses, from all directions. Butterflies small and butterflies large; butterflies light and butterflies dark; butterflies blue, pink, crimson, green, gold-colour— *every* colour, and far, far more colours than you could possibly imagine.

They all settled down, round the sides of the grassy dining-table, and in another minute a number of small white butterflies appeared, carrying among them flower petals carefully rolled up, each containing a drop of liquid. One of these was presented to the king, and then one to the queen, who each sniffed at their petal for an instant, and then passed it on to the butterfly

See page 92

The garden seemed actually alive with butterflies

next them, whereupon fresh petals were handed to them, which they again passed on.

'What are they doing, cuckoo?' said Griselda; 'that's not *eating*.'

'It's their kind of eating,' he replied. 'They don't require any other kind of food than a sniff of perfume; and as there are perfumes extracted from every flower in Butterfly Land, and there are far more flowers than you could count between now and Christmas, you must allow there is plenty of variety of dishes.'

'Um-m,' said Griselda; 'I suppose there is. But all the same, cuckoo, it's a very good thing I'm not hungry, isn't it? May I pour the scent on my pocket-handkerchief when it comes round to me? I have my handkerchief here, you see. Isn't it nice that I brought it? It was under my pillow, and I wrapped it round my hand to open the shutter, for the hook scratched it once.'

'You may pour one drop on your handkerchief,' said the cuckoo, 'but not more. I shouldn't like the butterflies to think you greedy.'

But Griselda grew very tired of the scent feast long before all the petals had been passed round. The perfumes were very nice, certainly, but there were such quantities of them—double quantities in honour of the guest, of course! Griselda screwed up her handkerchief into a tight little ball, so that the one drop of scent should not escape from it, and then she kept sniffing at it impatiently, till at last the cuckoo asked her what was the matter.

H

'I am so tired of the feast,' she said. 'Do let us do something else, cuckoo.'

'It is getting rather late,' said the cuckoo. 'But see, Griselda, they are going to have an air-dance now.'

'What's that?' said Griselda.

'Look, and you'll see,' he replied.

Flocks and flocks of butterflies were rising a short way into the air, and there arranging themselves in bands according to their colours.

'Come up on to the bank,' said the cuckoo to Griselda, 'you'll see them better.'

Griselda climbed up the bank, and as from there she could look down on the butterfly show, she saw it beautifully. The long strings of butterflies twisted in and out of each other in the most wonderful way, like ribbons of every hue plaiting themselves and then in an instant unplaiting themselves again. Then the king and queen placed themselves in the centre, and round and round in moving circles twisted and untwisted the brilliant bands of butterflies.

It's like a kaleidoscope,' said Griselda; 'and now it's like those twisty-twirly dissolving views that papa took me to see once. It's *just* like them. Oh, how pretty! Cuckoo, are they doing it all on purpose to please me?'

'A good deal,' said the cuckoo. 'Stand up and clap your hands loud three times, to show them you're pleased.'

Griselda obeyed. 'Clap' number one—all the butterflies rose up into the air in a cloud; clap number two—they all fluttered and twirled and buzzed about, as if in the greatest excitement; clap number three—they all turned in Griselda's direction with a rush.

'They're going to kiss you, Griselda,' cried the cuckoo.

Griselda felt her breath going. Up above her was the vast feathery cloud of butterflies, fluttering, *rushing* down upon her.

'Cuckoo, cuckoo,' she screamed, 'they'll suffocate me. Oh, cuckoo!'

'Shut your eyes, and clap your hands loud, very loud,' called out the cuckoo.

And just as Griselda clapped her hands, holding her precious handkerchief between her teeth, she heard him give his usual cry: 'Cuckoo, cuckoo.'

Clap—where were they all?

Griselda opened her eyes—garden, butterflies, cuckoo, all had disappeared. She was in bed, and Dorcas was knocking at the door with the hot water.

'Miss Grizzel said I was to wake you at your usual time this morning, missie,' she said. 'I hope you don't feel too tired to get up.'

'Tired! I should think not,' replied Griselda. 'I was awake this morning ages before you, I can tell you, my dear Dorcas. Come here for a minute, Dorcas, please,' she went on. 'There now, sniff my hand-kerchief. What do you think of that?'

'It's beautiful,' said Dorcas. 'It's out of the big blue chinay bottle on your auntie's table, isn't it, missie?'

'Stuff and nonsense,' replied Griselda; 'it's scent of my own, Dorcas. Aunt Grizzel never had any like it in her life. There now! Please give me my slippers, I want to get up and look over my lessons for Mr Knee-breeches before he comes. Dear me,' she added to herself, as she was putting on her slippers, 'how pretty my feet did look with the blue butterfly shoes! It was very good of the cuckoo to take me there, but I don't think I shall ever wish to be a butterfly again, now I know how hard they work! But I'd like to do my lessons well to-day. I fancy it'll please the dear old cuckoo.'

VIII

MASTER PHIL

Who comes from the world of flowers?
Daisy and crocus, and sea-blue bell,
And violet shrinking in dewy cell—
Sly cells that know the secrets of night,
When earth is bathed in fairy light—
Scarlet, and blue, and golden flowers.

AND so Mr Kneebreeches had no reason to complain of his pupil that day.

And Miss Grizzel congratulated herself more heartily than ever on her wise management of children.

And Miss Tabitha repeated that Sister Grizzel might indeed congratulate herself.

And Griselda became gradually more and more convinced that the only way as yet discovered of getting through hard tasks is to set to work and do them; also, that grumbling, as things are at present arranged in this world, does not *always*, nor I may say *often*, do good; furthermore, that an ill-tempered child is not, on the whole, likely to be as much loved as a good-tempered one; lastly, that if you wait long enough, winter will go and spring will come.

For this was the case this year, after all! Spring had only been sleepy and lazy, and in such a case what could poor old winter do but fill the vacant post till she

came? Why he should be so scolded and reviled for
faithfully doing his best, as he often is, I really don't
know. Not that all the ill words he gets have much
effect on him—he comes again just as usual, whatever
we say of or to him. I suppose his feelings have long
ago been frozen up, or surely before this he would
have taken offence—well for us that he has not done
so!

But when the spring did come at last this year it
would be impossible for me to tell you how Griselda
enjoyed it. It was like new life to her as well as to the
plants and flowers and birds and insects. Hitherto,
you see, she had been able to see very little of the outside
of her aunt's house; and charming as the inside was, the
outside, I must say, was still 'charminger.' There
seemed no end to the little up-and-down paths and
alleys, leading to rustic seats and quaint arbours; no
limits to the little pine-wood, down into which led the
dearest little zigzaggy path you ever saw, all bordered
with snowdrops and primroses and violets, and later on
with periwinkles and wood anemones, and those bright,
starry, white flowers, whose name no two people agree
about.

This wood-path was the place, I think, which
Griselda loved the best. The bowling-green was certainly very delightful, and so was the terrace where
the famous roses grew; but lovely as the roses were (I
am speaking just now, of course, of later on in the
summer, when they were all in bloom), Griselda could
not enjoy them as much as the wild flowers, for she was

forbidden to gather or touch them, except with her funny round nose!

'You may *scent* them, my dear,' said Miss Grizzel, who was of opinion that smell was not a pretty word; 'but I cannot allow anything more.'

And Griselda did 'scent' them, I assure you. She burrowed her whole rosy face in the big ones; but gently, for she did not want to spoil them, both for her aunt's sake, and because, too, she had a greater regard for flowers now that she knew the secret of how they were painted, and what a great deal of trouble the butterflies take about them.

But after a while one grows tired of 'scenting' roses; and even the trying to walk straight across the bowling-green with her eyes shut, from the arbour at one side to the arbour exactly like it at the other, grew stupid, though no doubt it would have been capital fun with a companion to applaud or criticize.

So the wood-path became Griselda's favourite haunt. As the summer grew on, she began to long more than ever for a companion—not so much for play, as for someone to play with. She had lessons, of course, just as many as in the winter; but with the long days there seemed to come a quite unaccountable increase of play-time, and Griselda sometimes found it hang heavy on her hands. She had not seen or heard anything of the cuckoo either, save, of course, in his 'official capacity' of time-teller, for a very long time.

'I suppose,' she thought, 'he thinks I don't need amusing, now that the fine days are come and I can play in the garden; and certainly, if I had *anyone* to play with, the garden would be perfectly lovely.'

But, failing companions, she did the best she could for herself, and this was why she loved the path down into the wood so much.   There was a sort of mystery about it; it might have been the path leading to the cottage of Red Riding-hood's grandmother, or a path leading to fairyland itself.   There were all kinds of queer, nice, funny noises to be heard there—in one part of it especially, where Griselda made herself a seat of some moss-grown stones, and where she came so often that she got to know all the little flowers growing close round about, and even the particular birds whose nests were hard by.

She used to sit there and *fancy*—fancy that she heard the wood-elves chattering under their breath, or the little underground gnomes and kobolds hammering at their fairy forges.   And the tinkling of the brook in the distance sounded like the enchanted bells round the necks of the fairy kine, who are sent out to pasture sometimes on the upper world hillsides.   For Griselda's head was crammed full, perfectly full, of fairy lore; and the mandarins' country, and Butterfly Land, were quite as real to her as the everyday world about her.

But all this time she was not forgotten by the cuckoo, as you will see.

One day she was sitting in her favourite nest, feeling, notwithstanding the sunshine, and the flowers, and the soft sweet air, and the pleasant sounds all about, rather dull and lonely.   For though it was only May, it was really quite a hot day, and Griselda had been all the morning at her lessons, and had tried very hard, and done them very well, and now she felt as if she deserved some reward. Suddenly in the distance, she heard a well-known sound: 'Cuckoo, cuckoo.'

'Can that be the cuckoo?' she said to herself; and in a moment she felt sure that it must be. For, for some reason that I do not know enough about the habits of real 'flesh and blood' cuckoos to explain, that bird was not known in the neighbourhood where Griselda's aunts lived. Some twenty miles or so further south it was heard regularly, but all this spring Griselda had never caught the sound of its familiar note, and she now remembered hearing it never came to these parts.

So, 'It must be my cuckoo,' she said to herself. 'He must be coming out to speak to me. How funny! I have never seen him by daylight.'

She listened. Yes, again there it was: 'Cuckoo, cuckoo,' as plain as possible, and nearer than before.

'Cuckoo,' cried Griselda, 'do come and talk to me. It's such a long time since I have seen you, and I have nobody to play with.'

But there was no answer. Griselda held her breath to listen, but there was nothing to be heard.

'Unkind cuckoo!' she exclaimed. 'He is tricking me, I do believe; and to-day too, just when I was so dull and lonely.'

The tears came into her eyes, and she was beginning to think herself very badly used, when suddenly a rustling in the bushes beside her made her turn round, more

than half expecting to see the cuckoo himself.   But it
was not he.   The rustling went on for a minute or two
without anything making its appearance, for the bushes
were pretty thick just there, and anyone scrambling up
from the pine-wood below would have had rather hard
work to get through, and indeed for a very big person
such a feat would have been altogether impossible.

It was not a very big person, however, who was
causing all the rustling, and crunching of branches, and
general commotion, which now absorbed Griselda's
attention.   She sat watching for another minute in
perfect stillness, afraid of startling by the slightest
movement the squirrel or rabbit or creature of some
kind which she expected to see.   At last—was that a
squirrel or rabbit—that rosy, round face, with shaggy,
fair hair falling over the eager blue eyes, and a general
look of breathlessness and overheatedness and deter-
mination?

A squirrel or a rabbit!   No, indeed, but a very
sturdy, very merry, very ragged little boy.

'Where are that cuckoo?   Does *you* know?' were
the first words he uttered, as soon as he had fairly
shaken himself, though not by any means all his
clothes, free of the bushes (for ever so many pieces of
jacket and knickerbockers, not to speak of one boot
and half his hat, had been left behind on the way), and
found breath to say something.

Griselda stared at him for a moment without speaking.   She was so astonished.   It was months since she
had spoken to a child, almost since she had seen one,

'Where are that cuckoo? Does you know?'

and about children younger than herself she knew very little at any time, being the baby of the family at home, you see, and having only big brothers older than herself for playfellows.

'Who are you?' she said at last. 'What's your name, and what do you want?'

'My name's Master Phil, and I want that cuckoo,' answered the little boy. 'He camed up this way. I'm sure he did, for he called me all the way.'

'He's not here,' said Griselda, shaking her head; 'and this is my aunt's garden. No one is allowed to come here but friends of theirs. You had better go home; and you have torn your clothes so.'

'This aren't a garden,' replied the little fellow undauntedly, looking round him; 'this are a wood. There are bluebells and primroses here, and that shows it aren't a garden—not anybody's garden, I mean, with walls round, for nobody to come in.'

'But it *is*,' said Griselda, getting rather vexed. 'If it isn't a garden it's *grounds*, private grounds, and nobody should come without leave. This path leads down to the wood, and there's a door in the wall at the bottom to get into the lane. You may go down that way, little boy. No one comes scrambling up the way you did.'

'But I want to find the cuckoo,' said the little boy. 'I do so want to find the cuckoo.'

His voice sounded almost as if he were going to cry, and his pretty, hot, flushed face puckered up. Griselda's heart smote her; she looked at him more carefully. He was such a very little boy, after all; she did not like to be cross to him.

'How old are you?' she asked.

'Five and a bit.   I had a birthday after the summer, and if I'm good, nurse says perhaps I'll have one after next summer too.   Do you ever have birthdays?' he went on, peering up at Griselda.   'Nurse says she used to when she was young, but she never has any now.'

'*Have* you a nurse?' asked Griselda, rather surprised; for, to tell the truth, from 'Master Phil's' appearance, she had not felt at all sure what *sort* of little boy he was, or rather what sort of people he belonged to.

'Of course I have a nurse, and a mother too,' said the little boy, opening wide his eyes in surprise at the question.   'Haven't you?   Perhaps you're too big, though.   People leave off having nurses and mothers when they're big, don't they?   Just like birthdays.   But *I* won't.   I won't never leave off having a mother any way.   I don't care so much about nurse and birth-days, not *kite* so much.   Did you care when you had to leave off, when you got too big?'

'I hadn't to leave off because I got big,' said Griselda sadly.   'I left off when I was much littler than you,' she went on, unconsciously speaking as Phil would best understand her.   'My mother died.'

'I'm werry sorry,' said Phil; and the way in which he said it quite overcame Griselda's unfriendliness.   'But perhaps you've a nice nurse.   My nurse is rather nice; but she *will* 'cold me to-day, won't she?' he added, laughing, pointing to the terrible rents in his garments.

'These are my very oldestest things; that's a good thing, isn't it? Nurse says I don't look like Master Phil in these, but when I have on my blue welpet, then I look like Master Phil. I shall have my blue welpet when mother comes.'

'Is your mother away?' said Griselda.

'Oh yes, she's been away a long time; so nurse came here to take care of me at the farmhouse, you know. Mother was ill, but she's better now, and some day she'll come too.'

'Do you like being at the farmhouse? Have you anybody to play with?' said Griselda.

Phil shook his curly head. 'I never have anybody to play with,' he said. 'I'd like to play with you if you're not too big. And do you think you could help me to find the cuckoo?' he added insinuatingly.

'What do you know about the cuckoo?' said Griselda.

'He called me,' said Phil, 'he called me lots of times; and to-day nurse was busy, so I thought I'd come. And do you know,' he added mysteriously, 'I do believe the cuckoo's a fairy, and when I find him I'm going to ask him to show me the way to fairyland.'

'He says we must all find the way ourselves,' said Griselda, quite forgetting to whom she was speaking.

'*Does* he?' cried Phil, in great excitement. 'Do you know him, then? and have you asked him? Oh, do tell me.'

Griselda recollected herself. 'You couldn't understand,' she said. 'Some day perhaps I'll tell you—I mean if ever I see you again.'

'But I may see you again,' said Phil, settling himself down comfortably beside Griselda on her mossy stone. 'You'll let me come, won't you? I like to talk about fairies, and nurse doesn't understand. And if the cuckoo knows you, perhaps that's why he called me to come to play with you.'

'How did he call you?' asked Griselda.

'First,' said Phil gravely, 'it was in the night. I was asleep, and I had been wishing I had somebody to play with, and then I d'eamed of the cuckoo—such a nice d'eam. And when I woke up I heard him calling me, and I wasn't d'eaming then. And then when I was in the field he called me, but I *couldn't* find him, and nurse said "Nonsense." And to-day he called me again, so I camed up through the bushes. And mayn't I come again? Perhaps if we both tried together we could find the way to fairyland. Do you think we could?'

'I don't know,' said Griselda dreamily. 'There's a great deal to learn first, the cuckoo says.'

'Have you learnt a great deal?' (he called it 'a gate deal') asked Phil, looking up at Griselda with increased respect. '*I* don't know scarcely nothing. Mother was ill such a long time before she went away, but I know she wanted me to learn to read books. But nurse is too old to teach me.'

'Shall I teach you?' said Griselda. 'I can bring some of my old books and teach you here after I have done my own lessons.'

'And then mother *would* be surprised when she comes back,' said Master Phil, clapping his hands.

'Oh, *do*.   And when I've learnt to read a great deal, do you think the cuckoo would show us the way to fairy-land?'

'I don't think it was that sort of learning he meant,' said Griselda.   'But I dare say that would help.   I *think*,' she went on, lowering her voice a little, and look-ing down gravely into Phil's earnest eyes, 'I *think* he means mostly learning to be very good—very, *very* good, you know.'

'Gooder than you?' said Phil.

'Oh dear, yes; lots and lots gooder than me,' replied Griselda.

'*I* think you're very good,' observed Phil, in a paren-thesis.   Then he went on with his cross-questioning.

'Gooder than mother?'

'I don't know your mother, so how can I tell how good she is?' said Griselda.

'*I* can tell you,' said Phil importantly.   'She is just as good as—as good as—as good as *good*.   That's what she is.'

'You mean she couldn't be better,' said Griselda, smiling.

'Yes, that'll do, if you like.   Would that be good enough for us to be, do you think?'

'We must ask the cuckoo,' said Griselda.   'But I'm sure it would be a good thing for you to learn to read. You must ask your nurse to let you come here every afternoon that it's fine, and I'll ask my aunt.'

'I needn't ask nurse,' said Phil composedly; 'she'll never know where I am, and I needn't tell her.   She

See page 135

'*Are you all right? . . . I'm going pretty fast*'

doesn't care what I do, except tearing my clothes; and when she 'colds me, *I* don't care.'

'*That* isn't good, Phil,' said Griselda gravely. 'You'll never be as good as good if you speak like that.'

'What should I say, then? Tell me,' said the little boy submissively.

'You should ask nurse to let you come to play with me, and tell her I'm much bigger than you, and I won't let you tear your clothes. And you should tell her you're very sorry you've torn them to-day.'

'Very well,' said Phil, 'I'll say that. But, oh, see!' he exclaimed, darting off, 'there's a field-mouse! If only I could catch him!'

Of course he couldn't catch him, nor could Griselda either; very ready though she was to do her best. But it was great fun all the same, and the children laughed heartily and enjoyed themselves tremendously. And when they were tired they sat down again and gathered flowers for nosegays, and Griselda was surprised to find how clever Phil was about it. He was much quicker than she at spying out the prettiest blossoms, however hidden behind tree, or stone, or shrub. And he told her of all the best places for flowers near by, and where grew the largest primroses and the sweetest violets, in a way that astonished her.

'You're such a little boy,' she said; 'how do you know so much about flowers?'

'I've had no one else to play with,' he said innocently. 'And then, you know, the fairies are so fond of them.'

When Griselda thought it was time to go home, she

I

led little Phil down the wood-path, and through the
door in the wall opening on to the lane.

'Now you can find your way home without scrambling through any more bushes, can't you, Master Phil?'
she said.

'Yes, thank you, and I'll come again to that place
to-morrow afternoon, shall I?' asked Phil. 'I'll know
when—after I've had my dinner and raced three times
round the big field, then it'll be time. That's how it
was to-day.'

'I should think it would do if you *walked* three times
—or twice if you like—round the field. It isn't a good
thing to race just when you've had your dinner,'
observed Griselda sagely. 'And you mustn't try to
come if it isn't fine, for my aunts won't let me go out if
it rains even the tiniest bit. And of course you must
ask your nurse's leave.'

'Very well,' said little Phil, as he trotted off. 'I'll
try to remember all those things. I'm so glad you'll
play with me again; and if you see the cuckoo, please
thank him.'

IX

Up and Down the Chimney

Helper. Well, but if it was all dream it would be the same as if it was all real, would it not?

Keeper. Yes, I see. I mean, sir, I do *not* see.

A Lilliput Revel.

NOT having 'just had her dinner,' and feeling very much inclined for her tea, Griselda ran home at a great rate.

She felt, too, in such good spirits; it had been so delightful to have a companion in her play.

'What a good thing it was I didn't make Phil run away before I found out what a nice little boy he was,' she said to herself. 'I must look out my old reading books to-night. I shall so like teaching him, poor little boy, and the cuckoo will be pleased at my doing something useful, I'm sure.'

Tea was quite ready, in fact waiting for her, when she came in. This was a meal she always had by herself, brought up on a tray to Dorcas's little sitting-room, where Dorcas waited upon her. And sometimes when Griselda was in a particularly good humour she would beg Dorcas to sit down and have a cup of tea with her —a liberty the old servant was far too dignified and respectful to have thought of taking, unless specially requested to do so.

This evening, as you know, Griselda was in a very particularly good humour, and besides this, so very full of her adventures, that she would have been glad of an even less sympathizing listener than Dorcas was likely to be.

'Sit down, Dorcas, and have some more tea, do,' she said coaxingly. 'It looks ever so much more comfortable, and I'm sure you could eat a little more if you tried, whether you've had your tea in the kitchen or not. I'm *fearfully* hungry, I can tell you. You'll have to cut a whole lot more bread and butter, and not "ladies' slices" either.'

'How your tongue does go, to be sure, Miss Griselda,' said Dorcas, smiling, as she seated herself on the chair Griselda had drawn in for her.

'And why shouldn't it?' said Griselda saucily. 'It doesn't do it any harm. But oh, Dorcas, I've had such fun this afternoon—really, you couldn't guess what I've been doing.'

'Very likely not, missie,' said Dorcas.

'But you might try to guess. Oh no, I don't think you need—guessing takes such a time, and I want to tell you. Just fancy, Dorcas, I've been playing with a little boy in the wood.'

'Playing with a little boy, Miss Griselda!' exclaimed Dorcas, aghast.

'Yes, and he's coming again to-morrow, and the day after, and every day, I dare say,' said Griselda. 'He *is* such a nice little boy.'

'But, missie,' began Dorcas.

'Well? What's the matter? You needn't look like that—as if I had done something naughty,' said Griselda sharply.

'But you'll tell your aunt, missie?'

'Of course,' said Griselda, looking up fearlessly into Dorcas's face with her bright grey eyes. 'Of course; why shouldn't I? I must ask her to give the little boy leave to come into *our* grounds; and I told the little boy to be sure to tell his nurse, who takes care of him, about his playing with me.'

'His nurse,' repeated Dorcas, in a tone of some relief. 'Then he must be quite a little boy; perhaps Miss Grizzel would not object so much in that case.'

'Why should she object at all? She might know I wouldn't want to play with a naughty rude boy,' said Griselda.

'She thinks all boys rude and naughty, I'm afraid, missie,' said Dorcas. 'All, that is to say, excepting your dear papa. But then, of course, she had the bringing up of *him* in her own way from the beginning.'

'Well, I'll ask her, any way,' said Griselda, 'and if she says I'm not to play with him, I shall think—I know what I shall *think* of Aunt Grizzel, whether I *say* it or not.'

And the old look of rebellion and discontent settled down again on her rosy face.

'Be careful, missie, now do, there's a dear good girl,' said Dorcas anxiously, an hour later, when Griselda, dressed as usual in her little white muslin frock, was ready to join her aunts at dessert.

But Griselda would not condescend to make any reply.

'Aunt Grizzel,' she said suddenly, when she had eaten an orange and three biscuits and drunk half a glass of home-made elderberry wine. 'Aunt Grizzel, when I was out in the garden to-day—down the wood-path, I mean—I met a little boy, and he played with me, and I want to know if he may come every day to play with me.'

Griselda knew she was not making her request in a very amiable or becoming manner; she knew, indeed, that she was making it in such a way as was almost certain to lead to its being refused; and yet, though she was really so very, very anxious to get leave to play with little Phil, she took a sort of spiteful pleasure in injuring her own cause.

How *foolish* ill temper makes us! Griselda had allowed herself to get so angry at the *thought* of being thwarted that had her aunt looked up quietly and said at once: 'Oh yes, you may have the little boy to play with you whenever you like,' she would really, in a strange distorted sort of way, have been *disappointed*.

But, of course, Miss Grizzel made no such reply. Nothing less than a miracle could have made her answer Griselda otherwise than as she did. Like Dorcas, for an instant, she was utterly 'flabbergasted,' if you know what that means. For she was really quite an old lady, you know, and sensible as she was, things upset her much more easily than when she was younger.

Naughty Griselda saw her uneasiness, and enjoyed it.

'Playing with a boy!' exclaimed Miss Grizzel. 'A boy in my grounds, and you, my niece, to have played with him!'

'Yes,' said Griselda coolly, 'and I want to play with him again.'

'Griselda,' said her aunt, 'I am too astonished to say more at present. Go to bed.'

'Why should I go to bed? It is not my bed-time,' cried Griselda, blazing up. 'What have I done to be sent to bed as if I were in disgrace?'

'Go to bed,' repeated Miss Grizzel. 'I will speak to you to-morrow.'

'You are very unfair and unjust,' said Griselda, starting up from her chair. 'That's all the good of being honest and telling everything. I might have played with the little boy every day for a month and you would never have known, if I hadn't told you.'

She banged across the room as she spoke, and out at the door, slamming it behind her rudely. Then upstairs like a whirlwind; but when she got to her own room she sat down on the floor and burst into tears, and when Dorcas came up, nearly half an hour later, she was still in the same place, crouched up in a little heap, sobbing bitterly.

'Oh, missie, missie,' said Dorcas, 'it's just what I was afraid of!'

As Griselda rushed out of the room Miss Grizzel leant back in her chair and sighed deeply.

'Already,' she said faintly. 'She was never so violent before. Can one afternoon's companionship with rudeness have already contaminated her? Already, Tabitha—can it be so?'

'Already,' said Miss Tabitha softly, shaking her head, which somehow made her look wonderfully like an old cat, for she felt cold of an evening and usually wore a very fine woolly shawl of a delicate grey shade, and the borders of her cap and the ruffles round her throat and wrists were all of fluffy, downy white. 'Already,' she said.

'Yet,' said Miss Grizzel, recovering herself a little, 'it is true what the child said. She might have deceived us. Have I been hard upon her, Sister Tabitha?'

'Hard upon her! Sister Grizzel,' said Miss Tabitha with more energy than usual. 'No, certainly not. For once, Sister Grizzel, I disagree with you. Hard upon her! Certainly not.'

But Miss Grizzel did not feel happy.

When she went up to her own room at night she was surprised to find Dorcas waiting for her, instead of the younger maid.

'I thought you would not mind having me, instead of Martha, to-night, ma'am,' she said, 'for I did so want to speak to you about Miss Griselda. The poor, dear young lady has gone to bed so very unhappy.'

'But do you know what she has done, Dorcas?' said Miss Grizzel. 'Admitted a *boy*, a rude, common, impertinent *boy*, unto my precincts, and played with him —with a *boy*, Dorcas.'

'Yes, ma'am,' said Dorcas. 'I know all about it,

Griselda rushed out of the room

ma'am. Miss Griselda has told me all. But if you would allow me to give an opinion, it isn't quite so bad. He's only a little boy, ma'am—between five and six— only just about the age Miss Griselda's dear papa was when he first came to us, and, by all I can hear, quite a little gentleman.'

'A little gentleman,' repeated Miss Grizzel, 'and not six years old! That is less objectionable than I expected. What is his name, as you know so much, Dorcas?'

'Master Phil,' replied Dorcas. 'That is what he told Miss Griselda, and she never thought to ask him more. But I'll tell you how we could get to hear more about him, I think, ma'am. From what Miss Griselda says, I believe he is staying at Mr Crouch's farm, and that, you know, ma'am, belongs to my Lady Lavander, though it is a good way from Merrybrow Hall. My lady is pretty sure to know about the child, for she knows all that goes on among her tenants, and I remember hearing that a little gentleman and his nurse had come to Mr Crouch's to lodge for six months.'

Miss Grizzel listened attentively.

'Thank you, Dorcas,' she said, when the old servant had left off speaking. 'You have behaved with your usual discretion. I shall drive over to Merrybrow to-morrow and make inquiry. And you may tell Miss Griselda in the morning what I purpose doing; but tell her also that, as a punishment for her rudeness and ill temper, she must have breakfast in her own room to-morrow, and not see me till I send for her. Had she restrained her temper and explained the matter, all this distress might have been saved.'

Dorcas did not wait till 'to-morrow morning'; she could not bear to think of Griselda's unhappiness. From her mistress's room she went straight to the little girl's, going in very softly, so as not to disturb her should she be sleeping.

'Are you awake, missie?' she said gently.

Griselda started up.

'Yes!' she exclaimed. 'Is it you, cuckoo? I'm quite awake.'

'Bless the child,' said Dorcas to herself, 'how her head does run on Miss Sybilla's cuckoo. It's really wonderful. There's more in such things than some people think.'

But aloud she only replied:

'It's Dorcas, missie. No fairy, only old Dorcas come to comfort you a bit. Listen, missie. Your auntie is going over to Merrybrow Hall to-morrow to inquire about this little Master Phil from my Lady Lavander, for we think it's at one of her ladyship's farms that he and his nurse are staying, and if she hears that he's a nice-mannered little gentleman, and comes of good parents—why, missie, there's no saying but that you'll get leave to play with him as much as you like.'

'But not to-morrow, Dorcas,' said Griselda. 'Aunt Grizzel never goes to Merrybrow till the afternoon. She won't be back in time for me to play with Phil to-morrow.'

'No, but next day, perhaps,' said Dorcas.

'Oh, but that won't do,' said Griselda, beginning to cry again. 'Poor little Phil will be coming up to the wood-path *to-morrow*, and if he doesn't find me he'll be *so* unhappy—perhaps he'll never come again if I don't meet him to-morrow.'

Dorcas saw that the little girl was worn out and excited, and not yet inclined to take a reasonable view of things.

'Go to sleep, missie,' she said kindly, 'and don't think anything more about it till to-morrow. It'll be all right, you'll see.'

Her patience touched Griselda.

'You are very kind, Dorcas,' she said. 'I don't mean to be cross to *you*; but I can't bear to think of poor little Phil. Perhaps he'll sit down on my mossy stone and cry. Poor little Phil!'

But notwithstanding her distress, when Dorcas had left her she did feel her heart a little lighter, and somehow or other before long she fell asleep.

When she awoke it seemed to be suddenly, and she had the feeling that something had disturbed her. She lay for a minute or two perfectly still—listening. Yes; there it was—the soft, faint rustle in the air that she knew so well. It seemed as if something was moving away from her.

'Cuckoo,' she said gently, 'is that you?'

A moment's pause, then came the answer—the pretty greeting she expected.

'Cuckoo, cuckoo,' soft and musical. Then the cuckoo spoke.

'Well, Griselda,' he said, 'and how are you? It's a good while since we have had any fun together.'

'That's not *my* fault,' said Griselda sharply. She was not yet feeling quite as amiable as might have been desired, you see. That's *certainly* not my fault,' she repeated.

'*One should always* walk *up to conclusions* . . .'

'I never said it was,' replied the cuckoo. 'Why will you jump at conclusions so? It's a very bad habit, for very often you jump *over* them, you see, and go too far. One should always *walk* up to conclusions, very slowly and evenly, right foot first, then left, one with another —that's the way to get where you want to go, and feel sure of your ground. Do you see?'

'I don't know whether I do or not, and I'm not going to speak to you if you go on at me like that. You might see I don't want to be lectured when I am so unhappy.'

'What are you unhappy about?'

'About Phil, of course. I won't tell you, for I believe you know,' said Griselda. 'Wasn't it you that sent him to play with me? I was so pleased, and I thought it was very kind of you; but it's all spoilt now.'

'But I heard Dorcas saying that your aunt is going over to consult my Lady Lavander about it,' said the cuckoo. 'It'll be all right; you needn't be in such low spirits about nothing.'

'Were you in the room *then?*' said Griselda. 'How funny you are, cuckoo. But it isn't all right. Don't you see, poor little Phil will be coming up the wood-path to-morrow afternoon to meet me, and I won't be there! I can't bear to think of it.'

'Is that all?' said the cuckoo. 'It really is extraordinary how some people make troubles out of nothing! We can easily tell Phil not to come till the day after. Come along.'

'Come along,' repeated Griselda. 'What do you mean?'

'Oh, I forgot,' said the cuckoo. 'You don't understand. Put out your hand. There, do you feel me?'

'Yes,' said Griselda, stroking gently the soft feathers which seemed to be close under her hand. 'Yes, I feel you.'

'Well, then,' said the cuckoo, 'put your arms round my neck, and hold me firm. I'll lift you up.'

'How *can* you talk such nonsense, cuckoo?' said Griselda. 'Why, one of my little fingers would clasp your neck. How can I put my arms round it?'

'Try,' said the cuckoo.

Somehow Griselda had to try.

She held out her arms in the cuckoo's direction, as if she expected his neck to be about the size of a Shetland pony's, or a large Newfoundland dog's; and, to her astonishment, so it was! A nice, comfortable, feathery neck it felt—so soft that she could not help laying her head down upon it, and nestling in the downy cushion.

'That's right,' said the cuckoo.

Then he seemed to give a little spring, and Griselda felt herself altogether lifted on to his back. She lay there as comfortably as possible—it felt so firm as well as soft. Up he flew a little way—then stopped short.

'Are you all right?' he inquired. 'You're not afraid of falling off?'

'Oh no,' said Griselda, 'not a bit.'

'You needn't be,' said the cuckoo, 'for you couldn't if you tried. I'm going on, then.'

'Where to?' said Griselda.

'Up the chimney first,' said the cuckoo.

'But there'll never be room,' said Griselda. 'I might *perhaps* crawl up like a sweep, hands and knees, you know, like going up a ladder. But stretched out

like this—it's just as if I were lying on a sofa—I *couldn't*
go up the chimney.'

'Couldn't you?' said the cuckoo. 'We'll see. *I*
intend to go, any way, and to take you with me. Shut
your eyes—one, two, three—here goes—we'll be up
the chimney before you know.'

They were floating about above the top of the house ...

It was quite true. Griselda shut her eyes tight. She
felt nothing but a pleasant sort of rush. Then she
heard the cuckoo's voice, saying:

'Well, wasn't that well done? Open your eyes and
look about you.'

Griselda did so. Where were they?

They were floating about above the top of the house,
which Griselda saw down below them, looking dark and
vast. She felt confused and bewildered.

'Cuckoo,' she said, 'I don't understand. Is it I that
have grown little, or you that have grown big?'

'Whichever you please,' said the cuckoo. 'You

have forgotten. I told you long ago it is all a matter of fancy.'

'Yes, if everything grew little *together*,' persisted Griselda; 'but it isn't everything. It's just you or me, or both of us. No, it can't be both of us. And I don't think it can be me, for if any of me had grown little all would, and my eyes haven't grown little, for everything looks as big as usual, only *you* a great deal bigger. My eyes can't have grown bigger without the rest of me, surely, for the moon looks just the same. And I must have grown little, or else we couldn't have got up the chimney. Oh, cuckoo, you have put all my thinking into such a muddle!'

'Never mind,' said the cuckoo. 'It'll show you how little consequence big and little are of. Make yourself comfortable all the same. Are you all right? Shut your eyes if you like. I'm going pretty fast.'

'Where to?' said Griselda.

'To Phil, of course,' said the cuckoo. 'What a bad memory you have! Are you comfortable?'

'*Very*, thank you,' replied Griselda, giving the cuckoo's neck an affectionate hug as she spoke.

'That'll do, thank you. Don't throttle me, if it's quite the same to you,' said the cuckoo. 'Here goes— one, two, three,' and off he flew again.

Griselda shut her eyes and lay still. It was delicious —the gliding, yet darting motion, like nothing she had ever felt before. It did not make her the least giddy, either; but a slightly sleepy feeling came over her. She felt no inclination to open her eyes; and, indeed, at the

K

rate they were going she could have distinguished very little had she done so.

Suddenly the feeling in the air about her changed. For an instant it felt more *rushy* than before, and there was a queer, dull sound in her ears. Then she felt that the cuckoo had stopped.

'Where are we?' she asked.

'We've just come *down* a chimney again,' said the cuckoo. 'Open your eyes and clamber down off my back, but don't speak loud, or you'll waken him, and that wouldn't do. There you are—the moonlight's coming in nicely at the window—you can see your way.'

Griselda found herself in a little bedroom, quite a tiny one, and by the look of the simple furniture and the latticed window, she saw that she was not in a grand house. But everything looked very neat and nice, and on a little bed in one corner lay a lovely sleeping child. It was Phil! He looked so pretty asleep—his shaggy curls all tumbling about, his rosy mouth half open as if smiling, one little hand tossed over his head, the other tight clasping a little basket which he had insisted on taking to bed with him, meaning as soon as he was dressed the next morning to run out and fill it with flowers for the little girl he had made friends with.

Griselda stepped up to the side of the bed on tiptoe. The cuckoo had disappeared, but Griselda heard his voice. It seemed to come from a little way up the chimney.

'Don't wake him,' said the cuckoo, 'but whisper

what you want to say into his ear, as soon as I have called him. He'll understand; he's accustomed to my ways.'

Then came the old note, soft and musical as ever:

'Cuckoo, cuckoo, cuckoo. Listen, Phil,' said the cuckoo, and without opening his eyes a change passed over the little boy's face. Griselda could see that he was listening to hear her message.

'He thinks he's dreaming, I suppose,' she said to herself with a smile. Then she whispered softly:

'Phil, dear, don't come to play with me to-morrow, for I can't come. But come the day after. I'll be at the wood-path then.'

'Welly well,' murmured Phil. Then he put out his two arms towards Griselda, all without opening his eyes, and she, bending down, kissed him softly.

'Phil's so sleepy,' he whispered, like a baby almost. Then he turned over and went to sleep more soundly than before.

'That'll do,' said the cuckoo. 'Come along, Griselda.'

Griselda obediently made her way to the place whence the cuckoo's voice seemed to come.

'Shut your eyes and put your arms round my neck again,' said the cuckoo.

She did not hesitate this time. It all happened just as before. There came the same sort of rushy sound; then the cuckoo stopped, and Griselda opened her eyes.

They were up in the air again—a good way up, too, for some grand old elms that stood beside the farm-house were gently waving their topmost branches a yard or two from where the cuckoo was poising himself and Griselda.

'Where shall we go to now?' he said. 'Or would you rather go home? Are you tired?'

'Tired!' exclaimed Griselda. 'I should rather think not. How could I be tired, cuckoo?'

'Very well, don't excite yourself about nothing, whatever you do,' said the cuckoo. 'Say where you'd like to go.'

'How can I?' said Griselda. 'You know far more nice places than I do.'

'You don't care to go back to the mandarins, or the butterflies, I suppose?' asked the cuckoo.

'No, thank you,' said Griselda. 'I'd like something new. And I'm not sure that I care for seeing any more countries of that kind, unless you could take me to the *real* fairyland.'

'*I* can't do that, you know,' said the cuckoo.

Just then a faint 'soughing' sound among the branches suggested another idea to Griselda.

'Cuckoo!' she exclaimed, 'take me to the sea. It's *such* a time since I saw the sea. I can fancy I hear it; do take me to see it.'

X

The Other Side of the Moon

That after supper time has come,
And silver dews the meadow steep,
And all is silent in the home,
And even nurses are asleep,
That be it late, or be it soon,
Upon this lovely night in June
They both will step into the moon.

'Very well,' said the cuckoo. 'You would like to look about you a little on the way, perhaps, Griselda, as we shall not be going down chimneys, or anything of that kind just at present.'

'Yes,' said Griselda. 'I think I should. I'm rather tired of shutting my eyes, and I'm getting quite accustomed to flying about with you, cuckoo.'

'Turn on your side, then,' said the cuckoo, 'and you won't have to twist your neck to see over my shoulder. Are you comfortable now? And, by the by, as you may be cold, just feel under my left wing. You'll find the feather mantle there, that you had on once before. Wrap it round you. I tucked it in at the last moment, thinking you might want it.'

'Oh, you dear, kind cuckoo!' cried Griselda. 'Yes, I've found it. I'll tuck it all round me like a rug— that's it. I *am* so warm now, cuckoo.'

'Here goes, then,' said the cuckoo, and off they set. Had ever a little girl such a flight before? Floating, darting, gliding, sailing—no words can describe it. Griselda lay still in delight, gazing all about her.

'How lovely the stars are, cuckoo!' she said. 'Is it true they're all great, big *suns*? I'd rather they weren't. I like to think of them as nice, funny little things.'

'They're not all suns,' said the cuckoo. 'Not all those you're looking at now.'

'I like the twinkling ones best,' said Griselda. 'They look so good-natured. Are they *all* twirling about always, cuckoo? Mr Kneebreeches has just begun to teach me astronomy, and *he* says they are; but I'm not at all sure that he knows much about it.'

'He's quite right all the same,' replied the cuckoo.

'Oh dear me! How tired they must be, then!' said Griselda. 'Do they never rest just for a minute?'

'Never.'

'Why not?'

'Obeying orders,' replied the cuckoo.

Griselda gave a little wriggle.

'What's the use of it?' she said. 'It would be just as nice if they stood still now and then.'

'Would it?' said the cuckoo. 'I know somebody who would soon find fault if they did. What would you say to no summer; no day, or no night, whichever it happened not to be, you see; nothing growing, and nothing to eat before long? That's what it would be if they stood still, you see, because——'

'Thank you, cuckoo,' interrupted Griselda. 'It's very nice to hear you—I mean, very dreadful to think of, but I don't want you to explain. I'll ask Mr Knee-breeches when I'm at my lessons. You might tell me one thing, however. What's at the other side of the moon?'

'There's a variety of opinions,' said the cuckoo.

'What are they? Tell me the funniest.'

'Some say all the unfinished work of the world is kept there,' said the cuckoo.

'*That*'s not funny,' said Griselda. 'What a messy place it must be! Why, even *my* unfinished work makes quite a heap. I don't like that opinion at all, cuckoo. Tell me another.'

'I have heard,' said the cuckoo, 'that among the places there you would find the country of the little black dogs. You know what sort of creatures those are?'

'Yes, I suppose so,' said Griselda, rather reluctantly.

'There are a good many of them in this world, as of course you know,' continued the cuckoo. 'But up there, they are much worse than here. When a child has made a great pet of one down here, I've heard tell the fairies take him up there when his parents and nurses think he's sleeping quietly in his bed, and make him work hard all night, with his own particular little black dog on his back. And it's so dreadfully heavy— for every time he takes it on his back down here it grows a pound heavier up there—that by morning the child is quite worn out. I dare say you've noticed how haggard and miserable some ill-tempered children get to look—now you'll know the reason.'

'Thank you, cuckoo,' said Griselda again; 'but I can't say I like this opinion about the other side of the moon any better than the first. If you please, I would rather not talk about it any more.'

'Oh, but it's not so bad an idea after all,' said the cuckoo. 'Lots of children, they say, get quite cured in the country of the little black dogs. It's this way— for every time a child refuses to take the dog on his back down here it grows a pound lighter up there, so at last any sensible child learns how much better it is to have nothing to say to it at all, and gets out of the way of it, you see. Of course, there *are* children whom nothing would cure, I suppose. What becomes of them I really can't say. Very likely they get crushed into pancakes by the weight of the dogs at last, and then nothing more is ever heard of them.'

'Horrid!' said Griselda, with a shudder. 'Don't let's talk about it any more, cuckoo; tell me your *own* opinion about what there really is on the other side of the moon.'

The cuckoo was silent for a moment. Then suddenly he stopped short in the middle of his flight.

'Would you like to see for yourself, Griselda?' he said. 'There would be about time to do it,' he added to himself, 'and it would fulfil her other wish, too.'

'See the moon for myself, do you mean?' cried Griselda, clasping her hands. 'I should rather think I would. Will you really take me there, cuckoo?'

'To the other side,' said the cuckoo. 'I couldn't take you to this side.'

'Why not? Not that I'd care to go to this side as much as to the other; for, of course, we can *see* this side from here. But I'd like to know why you couldn't take me there.'

'For *reasons*,' said the cuckoo dryly. 'I'll give you one if you like. If I took you to this side of the moon you wouldn't be yourself when you got there.'

'Who would I be, then?'

'Griselda,' said the cuckoo, 'I told you once that there are a great many things you don't know. Now, I'll tell you something more. There are a great many things you're not *intended* to know.'

'Very well,' said Griselda. 'But do tell me when you're going on again, and where you are going to take me to. There's no harm my asking that?'

'No,' said the cuckoo. 'I'm going on immediately, and I'm going to take you where you wanted to go to, only you must shut your eyes again, and lie perfectly still without talking, for I must put on steam—a good deal of steam—and I can't talk to you. Are you all right?'

'All right,' said Griselda.

She had hardly said the words when she seemed to fall asleep. The rushing sound in the air all round her increased so greatly that she was conscious of nothing else. For a moment or two she tried to remember where she was, and where she was going, but it was useless. She forgot everything, and knew nothing more of what was passing till—till she heard the cuckoo again.

'Cuckoo, cuckoo!   Wake up, Griselda,' he said.

Griselda sat up.

Where was she?

Not certainly where she had been when she went to sleep.   Not on the cuckoo's back, for there he was standing beside her, as tiny as usual.   Either he had grown little again or she had grown big—which, she supposed, it did not much matter.   Only it was very queer!

'Where am I, cuckoo?' she said.

'Where you wished to be,' he replied.   'Look about you and see.'

Griselda looked about her.   What did she see? Something that I can only give you a faint idea of, children; something so strange and unlike what she had ever seen before, that only in a dream could you see it as Griselda saw it.   And yet *why* it seemed to her so strange and unnatural I cannot well explain; if I could, my words would be as good as pictures, which I know they are not.

After all, it was only the sea she saw; but such a great, strange, silent sea, for there were no waves.   Griselda was seated on the shore, close beside the water's edge, but it did not come lapping up to her feet in the pretty, coaxing way that *our* sea does when it is in a good humour.   There were here and there faint ripples on the surface, caused by the slight breezes which now and then came softly round Griselda's face, but that was all.

King Canute might have sat 'from then till now' by this still, lifeless ocean without the chance of reading his silly attendants a lesson—if, indeed, there ever were such silly people, which I very much doubt.

Griselda gazed with all her eyes.   Then she suddenly gave a little shiver.

'What's the matter?' said the cuckoo.   'You have the mantle on—you're not cold?'

'No,' said Griselda, 'I'm not cold; but somehow, cuckoo, I feel a little frightened.   The sea is so strange, and so dreadfully big; and the light is so queer, too. What is the light, cuckoo?   It isn't moonlight, is it?'

'Not exactly,' said the cuckoo.   'You can't both have your cake and eat it, Griselda.   Look up at the sky.   There's no moon there, is there?'

'No,' said Griselda; 'but what lots of stars, cuckoo. The light comes from them, I suppose?   And where's the sun, cuckoo?   Will it be rising soon?   It isn't always like this up here, is it?'

'Bless you, no,' said the cuckoo.   'There's sun enough, and rather too much, sometimes.   How would you like a day a fortnight long, and nights to match? If it had been daytime here just now, I couldn't have brought you.   It's just about the very middle of the night now, and in about a week of *your* days the sun will begin to rise, because, you see——'

'Oh, *dear* cuckoo, please don't explain!' cried Griselda.   'I'll promise to ask Mr Kneebreeches, I will indeed.   In fact, he was telling me something just like it to-day or yesterday—which should I say?—at my astronomy lesson. And that makes it so strange that you should have brought me up here to-night to see for myself, doesn't it, cuckoo?'

'An odd coincidence,' said the cuckoo.

'What *would* Mr Kneebreeches think if I told him where I had been?' continued Griselda. 'Only, you see, cuckoo, I never tell anybody about what I see when I am with you.'

'No,' replied the cuckoo; 'better not. ("Not that you could if you tried," he added to himself.) You're not frightened now, Griselda, are you?'

'No, I don't think I am,' she replied. 'But, cuckoo, isn't this sea *awfully* big?'

'Pretty well,' said the cuckoo. 'Just half, or nearly half, the size of the moon; and, no doubt, Mr Knee-breeches has told you that the moon's diameter and circumference are respec——'

'Oh, *don't*, cuckoo!' interrupted Griselda, beseech-ingly. 'I want to enjoy myself, and not to have lessons. Tell me something funny, cuckoo. Are there any mermaids in the moon-sea?'

'Not exactly,' said the cuckoo.

'What a stupid way to answer,' said Griselda. 'There's no sense in that; there either must be or must not be. There couldn't be half mermaids.'

'I don't know about that,' replied the cuckoo. 'They might have been here once and have left their tails behind them, like Bo-peep's sheep, you know; and some day they might be coming to find them again, you know. That would do for "not exactly," wouldn't it?'

'*The sea is so strange, and so dreadfully big . . .*'

'Cuckoo, you're laughing at me,' said Griselda. 'Tell me, are there any mermaids, or fairies, or water-sprites, or any of those sort of creatures here?'

'I must still say "not exactly,"' said the cuckoo. 'There are beings here, or rather there have been, and there may be again; but you, Griselda, can know no more than this.'

His tone was rather solemn, and again Griselda felt a little 'eerie.'

'It's a dreadfully long way from home, any way,' she said. 'I feel as if, when I go back, I shall perhaps find I have been away fifty years or so, like the little boy in the fairy story. Cuckoo, I think I would like to go home. Mayn't I get on your back again?'

'Presently,' said the cuckoo. 'Don't be uneasy, Griselda. Perhaps I'll take you home by a short cut.'

'Was ever any child here before?' asked Griselda, after a little pause.

'Yes,' said the cuckoo.

'And did they get safe home again?'

'Quite,' said the cuckoo. 'It's so silly of you, Griselda, to have all these ideas still about far and near, and big and little, and long and short, after all I've taught you and all you've seen.'

'I'm very sorry,' said Griselda humbly; 'but you see, cuckoo, I can't help it. I suppose I'm made so.'

'Perhaps,' said the cuckoo meditatively.

He was silent for a minute. Then he spoke again. 'Look over there, Griselda,' he said. 'There's the short cut.'

Griselda looked.   Far, far over the sea, in the silent distance, she saw a tiny speck of light.   It was very tiny; but yet the strange thing was that, far away as it appeared, and minute as it was, it seemed to throw off a thread of light to Griselda's very feet—right across the great sheet of faintly gleaming water.   And as Griselda looked, the thread seemed to widen and grow, becoming at the same time brighter and clearer, till at last it lay before her like a path of glowing light.

'Am I to walk along there?' she said softly to the cuckoo.

'No,' he replied.   'Wait.'

Griselda waited, looking still, and presently in the middle of the shining streak she saw something slowly moving—something from which the light came, for the nearer it got to her the shorter grew the glowing path, and behind the moving object the sea looked no, brighter than before it had appeared.

At last—at last, it came quite near—near enough for Griselda to distinguish clearly what it was.

It was a little boat—the prettiest, the loveliest little boat that ever was seen; and it was rowed by a little figure that at first sight Griselda felt certain was a fairy.   For it was a child with bright hair and silvery wings, which with every movement sparkled and shone like a thousand diamonds.

Griselda sprang up and clapped her hands with delight.   At the sound, the child in the boat turned and looked at her.   For one instant she could not remember where she had seen him before; then she exclaimed joyfully:

'It is Phil! Oh, cuckoo, it is Phil. Have you turned into a fairy, Phil?'

But, alas, as she spoke the light faded away, the boy's figure disappeared, the sea and the shore and the sky were all as they had been before, lighted only by the faint, strange gleaming of the stars. Only the boat remained. Griselda saw it close to her, in the shallow water, a few feet from where she stood.

'Cuckoo,' she exclaimed in a tone of reproach and disappointment, 'where is Phil gone? Why did you send him away?'

'I didn't send him away,' said the cuckoo. 'You don't understand. Never mind, but get into the boat. It'll be all right, you'll see.'

'But are we to go away and leave Phil here, all alone at the other side of the moon?' said Griselda, feeling ready to cry.

'Oh, you silly girl!' said the cuckoo. 'Phil's all right, and in some ways he has a great deal more sense than you, I can tell you. Get into the boat and make yourself comfortable; lie down at the bottom and cover yourself up with the mantle. You needn't be afraid of wetting your feet a little, moon water never gives cold. There, now.'

Griselda did as she was told. She was beginning to feel rather tired, and it certainly was very comfortable at the bottom of the boat, with the nice warm feather mantle well tucked round her.

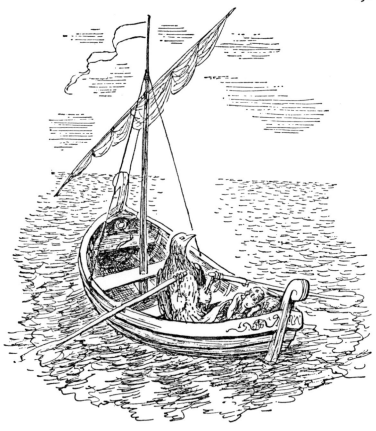

. . . she heard the soft dip, dip of the oars . . .

'Who will row?' she said sleepily. '*You* can't, cuckoo, with your tiny little claws, you could never hold the oars, I'm——'

'Hush!' said the cuckoo; and whether he rowed or not Griselda never knew.

L

Off they glided somehow, but it seemed to Griselda that *somebody* rowed, for she heard the soft dip, dip of the oars as they went along, so regularly that she couldn't help beginning to count in time—one, two, three, four—on, on—she thought she had got nearly to a hundred, when——

XI

'Cuckoo, Cuckoo, Good-bye!'

Children, try to be good!
  That is the end of all teaching;
Easily understood,
  And very easy in preaching.
And if you find it hard,
  Your efforts you need but double;
Nothing deserves reward
  Unless it has given us trouble.

—When she forgot everything, and fell fast, fast asleep, to wake, of course, in her own little bed as usual.

'One of your tricks again, Mr Cuckoo,' she said to herself with a smile. 'However, I don't mind. It *was* a short cut home, and it was very comfortable in the boat, and I certainly saw a great deal last night, and I'm very much obliged to you—particularly for making it all right with Phil about not coming to play with me to-day. Ah! that reminds me, I'm in disgrace. I wonder if Aunt Grizzel will really make me stay in my room all day. How tired I shall be, and what will Mr Kneebreeches think! But it serves me right. I *was* very cross and rude.'

There came a tap at the door. It was Dorcas with the hot water.

'Good morning, missie,' she said gently, not feeling, to tell the truth, very sure as to what sort of a humour 'missie' was likely to be found in this morning. 'I hope you've slept well.'

'Exceedingly well, thank you, Dorcas. I've had a delightful night,' replied Griselda amiably, smiling to herself at the thought of what Dorcas would say if she knew where she had been, and what she had been doing since last she saw her.

'That's good news,' said Dorcas in a tone of relief; 'and I've good news for you, too, missie. At least, I hope you'll think it so. Your aunt has ordered the carriage for quite early this morning—so you see she really wants to please you, missie, about playing with little Master Phil; and if to-morrow's a fine day, we'll be sure to find some way of letting him know to come.'

'Thank you, Dorcas. I hope it will be all right, and that Lady Lavander won't say anything against it. I dare say she won't. I feel ever so much happier this morning, Dorcas; and I'm very sorry I was so rude to Aunt Grizzel, for of course I know I *should* obey her.'

'That's right, missie,' said Dorcas approvingly.

'It seems to me, Dorcas,' said Griselda dreamily, when, a few minutes later, she was standing by the window while the old servant brushed out her thick, wavy hair, 'it seems to me, Dorcas, that it's *all* "obeying orders" together. There's the sun now, just getting up, and the moon just going to bed—*they* are always obeying, aren't they? I wonder why it should be so hard for people—for children, at least.'

'To be sure, missie, you do put it a way of your own,' replied Dorcas, somewhat mystified; 'but I see how you mean, I think, and it's quite true. And it *is* a hard lesson to learn.'

'I want to learn it *well*, Dorcas,' said Griselda, resolutely. 'So will you please tell Aunt Grizzel that I'm very sorry about last night, and I'll do just as she likes about staying in my room or anything. But, if she *would* let me, I'd far rather go down and do my lessons as usual for Mr Kneebreeches. I won't ask to go out in the garden; but I would like to please Aunt Grizzel by doing my lessons *very* well.'

Dorcas was both delighted and astonished. Never had she known her little 'missie' so altogether submissive and reasonable.

'I only hope the child's not going to be ill,' she said to herself. But she proved a skilful ambassadress, notwithstanding her misgivings; and Griselda's imprisonment confined her only to the bounds of the house and terrace walk, instead of within the four walls of her own little room, as she had feared.

Lessons *were* very well done that day, and Mr Kneebreeches's report was all that could be wished.

'I am particularly gratified,' he remarked to Miss Grizzel, 'by the intelligence and interest Miss Griselda displays with regard to the study of astronomy, which I have recently begun to give her some elementary instruction in. And, indeed, I have no fault to find with the way in which any of the young lady's tasks are performed.'

'I am extremely glad to hear it,' replied Miss Grizzel graciously, and the kiss with which she answered Griselda's request for forgiveness was a very hearty one.

And it was 'all right' about Phil.

'*I am particularly gratified . . .*'

Lady Lavander knew all about him; his father and mother were friends of hers, for whom she had a great regard, and for some time she had been intending to ask the little boy to spend the day at Merrybrow Hall, to be introduced to her god-daughter Griselda. So, *of course*, as Lady Lavander knew all about him, there could be no objection to his playing in Miss Grizzel's garden!

And 'to-morrow' turned out a fine day. So altogether you can imagine that Griselda felt very happy
and light-hearted as she ran down the wood-path to
meet her little friend, whose rosy face soon appeared
among the bushes.

'What did you do yesterday, Phil?' asked Griselda.
'Were you sorry not to come to play with me?'

'No,' said Phil mysteriously, 'I didn't mind. I was
looking for the way to fairyland to show you, and
I do believe I've found it. Oh, it *is* such a pretty
way.'

Griselda smiled.

'I'm afraid the way to fairyland isn't so easily found,'
she said. 'But I'd like to hear about where you went.
Was it far?'

'A good way,' said Phil. 'Won't you come with
me? It's in the wood. I can show you quite well,
and we can be back by tea-time.'

'Very well,' said Griselda; and off they set.

Whether it was the way to fairyland or not, it was not
to be wondered at that little Phil thought so. He led
Griselda right across the wood to a part where she had
never been before. It was pretty rough work part of
the way. The children had to fight with brambles and
bushes, and here and there to creep through on hands
and knees, and Griselda had to remind Phil several
times of her promise to his nurse that his clothes should
not be the worse for his playing with her, to prevent his
scrambling through 'anyhow' and leaving bits of his
knickerbockers behind him.

But when at last they reached Phil's favourite spot all their troubles were forgotten. Oh, how pretty it was! It was a sort of tiny glade in the very middle of the wood—a little green nest enclosed all round by trees, and right through it the merry brook came rippling along as if rejoicing at getting out into the sunlight again for a while. And all the choicest and sweetest of the early summer flowers seemed to be collected here in greater variety and profusion than in any other part of the wood.

'*Isn't* it nice?' said Phil, as he nestled down beside Griselda on the soft, mossy grass. 'It must have been a fairies' garden some time, I'm sure, and I shouldn't wonder if one of the doors into fairyland is hidden somewhere here, if only we could find it.'

'If only!' said Griselda. 'I don't think we shall find it, Phil; but, any way, this is a lovely place you've found, and I'd like to come here very often.'

Then at Phil's suggestion they set to work to make themselves a house in the centre of this fairies' garden, as he called it. They managed it very much to their own satisfaction, by dragging some logs of wood and big stones from among the brushwood hard by, and filling the holes up with bracken and furze.

'And if the fairies *do* come here,' said Phil, 'they'll be very pleased to find a house all ready, won't they?'

Then they had to gather flowers to ornament the house inside, and dry leaves and twigs all ready for a fire in one corner. Altogether it was quite a business, I can assure you, and when it was finished they were

very hot and very tired and *rather* dirty.   Suddenly a
thought struck Griselda.

'Phil,' she said, 'it must be getting late.'

'Past tea-time?' he said coolly.

'I dare say it is.   Look how low down the sun has
got.   Come, Phil, we must be quick.   Where is the
place we came out of the wood at?'

'Here,' said Phil, diving at a little opening among
the bushes.

Griselda followed him.   He had been a good guide
hitherto, and she certainly could not have found her
way alone.   They scrambled on for some way, then
the bushes suddenly seemed to grow less thick, and in a
minute they came out upon a little path.

'Phil,' said Griselda, 'this isn't the way we came.'

'Isn't it?' said Phil, looking about him.   'Then we
must have comed the wrong way.'

'I'm afraid so,' said Griselda, 'and it seems to be so
late already.   I'm so sorry, for Aunt Grizzel will be
vexed, and I did so want to please her.   Will your
nurse be vexed, Phil?'

'I don't care if she are,' replied Phil valiantly.

'You shouldn't say that, Phil.   You know we
shouldn't have stayed so long playing.'

'Nebber mind,' said Phil.   'If it was mother I
would mind.   Mother's so good, you don't know.
And she never 'colds me, except when I *am* naughty—
so I *do* mind.'

'She wouldn't like you to be out so late, I'm
sure,' said Griselda in distress, 'and it's most my

fault, for I'm the biggest.   Now, which way *shall* we
go?'

They had followed the little path till it came to a
point where two roads, rough cart-ruts only, met; or,
rather, where the path ran across the road.   Right, or
left, or straight on, which should it be?   Griselda stood
still in perplexity.   Already it was growing dusk;
already the moon's soft light was beginning faintly to
glimmer through the branches.   Griselda looked up
to the sky.

'To think,' she said to herself—'to think that I
should not know my way in a little bit of a wood like
this—I that was up at the other side of the moon last
night.'

The remembrance put another thought into her
mind.

'Cuckoo, cuckoo,' she said softly, 'couldn't you help
us?'

Then she stood still and listened, holding Phil's cold
little hands in her own.

She was not disappointed.   Presently, in the distance,
came the well-known cry: 'Cuckoo, cuckoo,' so soft
and far away, but yet so clear.

Phil clapped his hands.

'He's calling us,' he cried joyfully.   'He's going to
show us the way.   That's how he calls me always.
Good cuckoo, we're coming'; and, pulling Griselda
along, he darted down the road to the right—the
direction from whence came the cry.

They had some way to go, for they had wandered far

in a wrong direction, but the cuckoo never failed them.
Whenever they were at a loss—whenever the path
turned or divided, they heard his clear, sweet call; and,
without the least misgiving, they followed it, till at last
it brought them out upon the high road, a stone's
throw from Farmer Crouch's gate.

'I know the way now, good cuckoo,' exclaimed Phil.
'I can go home alone now, if your aunt will be vexed
with you.'

'No,' said Griselda, 'I must take you quite all the
way home, Phil dear.   I promised to take care of you,
and if nurse scolds anyone it must be me, not you.'

There was a little bustle about the door of the farm-
house as the children wearily came up to it.   Two or
three men were standing together receiving directions
from Mr Crouch himself and Phil's nurse was talking
eagerly.   Suddenly she caught sight of the truants.

'Here he is, Mr Crouch!' she exclaimed.   'No need
now to send to look for him.   Oh, Master Phil, how
could you stay out so late?   And to-night of all nights,
just when your—— I forgot, I mustn't say.   Come
into the parlour at once—and this little girl, who is
she?'

'She isn't a little girl, she's a young lady,' said Master
Phil, putting on his lordly air, 'and she's to come into
the parlour and have some supper with me, and then
someone must take her home to her auntie's house—
that's what I say.'

More to please Phil than from any wish for 'supper,'
for she was really in a fidget to get home, Griselda let

the little boy lead her into the parlour. But she was for a moment perfectly startled by the cry that broke from him when he opened the door and looked into the room. A lady was standing there, gazing out of the window, though in the quickly growing darkness she could hardly have distinguished the little figure she was watching for so anxiously.

The noise of the door opening made her look round.

'Phil,' she cried, 'my own little Phil; where have you been to? You didn't know I was waiting here for you, did you?'

'Mother, mother!' shouted Phil, darting into his mother's arms.

But Griselda drew back into the shadow of the doorway, and tears filled her eyes as for a minute or two she listened to the cooings and caressings of the mother and son.

Only for a minute, however. Then Phil called to her.

'Mother, mother,' he cried again, 'you must kiss Griselda, too! She's the little girl that is so kind, and plays with me; and she has no mother,' he added in a lower tone.

The lady put her arm round Griselda, and kissed her, too. She did not seem surprised.

'I think I know about Griselda,' she said very kindly, looking into her face with her gentle eyes, blue and clear like Phil's.

And then Griselda found courage to say how uneasy she was about the anxiety her aunts would be feeling,

'*I think I know about Griselda*'

and a messenger was sent off at once to tell of her being
safe at the farm.

But Griselda herself the kind lady would not lct go
till she had some nice supper with Phil, and was both
warmed and rested.

'And what were you about, children, to lose your
way?' she asked presently.

'I took Griselda to see a place that I thought was

the way to fairyland, and then we stayed to build a house for the fairies, in case they come, and then we came out at the wrong side, and it got dark,' explained Phil.

'And *was* it the way to fairyland?' asked his mother, smiling.

Griselda shook her head as she replied:

'Phil doesn't understand yet,' she said gently. 'He isn't old enough. The way to the true fairyland is hard to find, and we must each find it for ourselves, mustn't we?'

She looked up in the lady's face as she spoke, and saw that *she* understood.

'Yes, dear child,' she answered softly, and perhaps a very little sadly. 'But Phil and you may help each other, and I perhaps may help you both.'

Griselda slid her hand into the lady's. 'You're not going to take Phil away, are you?' she whispered.

'No, I have come to stay here,' she answered, 'and Phil's father is coming too, soon. We are going to live at the White House—the house on the other side of the wood, on the way to Merrybrow. Are you glad, children?'

.   .   .   .   .

Griselda had a curious dream that night—merely a dream, nothing else. She dreamt that the cuckoo came once more; this time, he told her, to say good-bye.

'For you will not need me now,' he said. 'I leave you in good hands, Griselda. You have friends now

who will understand you—friends who will help you
both to work and to play.   Better friends than the
mandarins, or the butterflies, or even than your faithful
old cuckoo.'

And when Griselda tried to speak to him, to thank
him for his goodness, to beg him still sometimes to come
to see her, he gently fluttered away.   'Cuckoo, cuckoo,
cuckoo,' he warbled; but somehow the last 'cuckoo'
sounded like 'good-bye.'

In the morning, when Griselda awoke, her pillow
was wet with tears.   Thus many stories end.   She was
happy, very happy in the thought of her kind new
friends; but there were tears for the one she felt she had
said farewell to, even though he was only a cuckoo in
a clock.

CHILDREN'S ILLUSTRATED CLASSICS
(Illustrated Classics for Older Readers are listed on fourth page)

FAIRY TALES FROM THE ARABIAN NIGHTS. Illustrated by KIDDELL-MONROE.
Here are the favourite tales—the fairy tales—out of the many told in the 'Thousand and One Nights'.

FAIRY TALES OF LONG AGO. Edited by M. C. CAREY. Illustrated by D. J. WATKINS-PITCHFORD.
This varied collection takes in translations from Charles Perrault, Madame de Beaumont, the Countess d'Aulnoy of France, Asbjörnsen and Moe, etc.

Selma Lagerlöf's **THE FURTHER ADVENTURES OF NILS.** Illustrated by HANS BAUMHAUER.
Nils's adventures continue with his flight over lake, hill, ice, snow, forest and moor of Sweden. The artist ably interprets the visual contrasts of the journey. (Not available in the U.S.A. in this edition.) *See also* THE WONDERFUL ADVENTURES OF NILS.

Louisa M. Alcott's **GOOD WIVES.** Illustrated by S. VAN ABBÉ, R.B.A., A.R.E.

Frances Browne's **GRANNY'S WONDERFUL CHAIR.** Illustrated by DENYS WATKINS-PITCHFORD.
The author, blind from birth, draws upon the Irish fairy-stories of her childhood to add magic and colour to the whole of this enchanting book.

GRIMMS' FAIRY TALES. Illustrated by CHARLES FOLKARD.

HANS ANDERSEN'S FAIRY TALES. Illustrated by HANS BAUMHAUER.
A new English rendering, including some new and outstanding tales.

Mary Mapes Dodge's **HANS BRINKER.** Illustrated by HANS BAUMHAUER.
This story is the best known and best loved work of the author.

Johanna Spyri's **HEIDI.** Illustrated by VINCENT O. COHEN.
This is the famous story of a Swiss child and her life among the Alps.

Charles Kingsley's **THE HEROES.** Illustrated by KIDDELL-MONROE.
A retelling of the legends of Perseus, the Argonauts and Theseus.

Louisa M. Alcott's **JO'S BOYS.** Illustrated by HARRY TOOTHILL.
'There is an abiding charm about the story.' *Scotsman.*

A. M. Hadfield's **KING ARTHUR AND THE ROUND TABLE.** Illustrated by DONALD SETON CAMMELL.
The haunting world of the Round Table.

Charlotte M. Yonge's **THE LITTLE DUKE.** Illustrated by MICHAEL GODFREY.
The story of Richard the Fearless, Duke of Normandy from 942 to 996.

Frances Hodgson Burnett's **LITTLE LORD FAUNTLEROY**
'The best version of the Cinderella story in a modern idiom that exists.'
MARGHANITA LASKI.

Louisa M. Alcott's **LITTLE MEN.** Illustrated by HARRY TOOTHILL.
Harry Toothill's drawings capture the liveliness of a young gentlemen's academy.

Louisa M. Alcott's **LITTLE WOMEN.** Illustrated by S. VAN ABBÉ.
S. van Abbé's drawings capture the vivacity and charm of the March family.

Mrs Ewing's **LOB LIE-BY-THE-FIRE and THE STORY OF A SHORT LIFE.** Illustrated by RANDOLPH CALDECOTT ('Lob') and H. M. BROCK ('Short Life'). Two of Mrs Ewing's most charming stories.

MODERN FAIRY STORIES. Edited by ROGER LANCELYN GREEN. Illustrated by E. H. SHEPARD.
Original (not 'retold') fairy stories by thirteen authors of modern times.

Jean Ingelow's MOPSA THE FAIRY. Illustrated by DORA CURTIS.
A river journey leads to the realms of wonder.

NURSERY RHYMES. Collected and illustrated in two-colour line by A. H. WATSON.
A comprehensive book of nursery rhymes.

Carlo Collodi's PINOCCHIO. The Story of a Puppet. Illustrated by CHARLES FOLKARD.
The most enchanting story of a puppet ever written.

Andrew Lang's PRINCE PRIGIO and PRINCE RICARDO. Illustrated by D. J. WATKINS-PITCHFORD.
Two modern fairy tales, rich in romantic adventures.

George MacDonald's THE LOST PRINCESS
THE PRINCESS AND CURDIE
THE PRINCESS AND THE GOBLIN
The first two volumes illustrated by CHARLES FOLKARD, the third by D. J. WATKINS-PITCHFORD.

Carola Oman's ROBIN HOOD. Illustrated by S. VAN ABBÉ.
Carola Oman lends substance to the 'Prince of Outlaws'.

W. M. Thackeray's THE ROSE AND THE RING and Charles Dickens's **THE MAGIC FISH-BONE.**
Two children's stories, the first containing the author's illustrations, the latter containing PAUL HOGARTH's work.

J. R. Wyss's THE SWISS FAMILY ROBINSON. Illustrated by CHARLES FOLKARD.
This is a new version by Audrey Clark of the popular classic.

Charles and Mary Lamb's TALES FROM SHAKESPEARE. Illustrated by ARTHUR RACKHAM.

TALES OF MAKE-BELIEVE. Edited by ROGER LANCELYN GREEN. Illustrated by HARRY TOOTHILL.
Charles Dickens, Rudyard Kipling, E. Nesbit, Thomas Hardy, E. V. Lucas, etc.

Nathaniel Hawthorne's TANGLEWOOD TALES. Illustrated by S. VAN ABBÉ.
This is a sequel to the famous *Wonder Book*.

Thomas Hughes's TOM BROWN'S SCHOOLDAYS. Illustrated by S. VAN ABBÉ.
'The best story of a boy's schooldays ever written.'

Charles Kingsley's THE WATER-BABIES. Illustrated by ROSALIE K. FRY.
The artist's drawings delicately interpret the fantastic beauty of the underwater world.

Nathaniel Hawthorne's A WONDER BOOK. Illustrated by S. VAN ABBÉ.
Hawthorne's famous *Wonder Book* recalls the immortal fables of antiquity.

Selma Lagerlöf's THE WONDERFUL ADVENTURES OF NILS. Illustrated by HANS BAUMHAUER.
Translated into most languages of the world, this Swedish tale of the boy who rode on the back of a young gander and flew northwards to find surprising adventures is a great favourite. (Not available in the U.S.A. in this edition.)
See also THE FURTHER ADVENTURES OF NILS.

Robert Louis Stevenson's THE BLACK ARROW. Illustrated by LIONEL EDWARDS.
The period is the England of the Wars of the Roses.

Charles Dickens's A CHRISTMAS CAROL and THE CRICKET ON THE HEARTH.
Illustrated by C. E. BROCK.

Illustrated Classics for Older Readers

Jean Webster's DADDY LONG-LEGS. Illustrated by HARRY FAIRBAIRN.
'An all-time favourite' and best-seller.

Ballantyne's THE DOG CRUSOE. Illustrated by VICTOR AMBRUS.
A man and his dog go on a peace mission to the Indian tribes.

Cervantes's DON QUIXOTE. Illustrated by W. HEATH ROBINSON.
An edition suitably edited from the Cervantes's original.

Jonathan Swift's GULLIVER'S TRAVELS. Illustrated by ARTHUR RACKHAM.
Gulliver's Travels is one of the great satires in the English language.

Robert Louis Stevenson's KIDNAPPED. Illustrated by G. OAKLEY.
A great adventure story and companion piece to *Treasure Island*.

H. Rider Haggard's KING SOLOMON'S MINES. Illustrated by A. R. WHITEAR.
A witch and treasure hunt in the heart of Africa.

R. D. Blackmore's LORNA DOONE. Illustrated by LIONEL EDWARDS.
An edition capturing the spirit of this evergreen romance.

John Bunyan's THE PILGRIM'S PROGRESS. Illustrated by FRANK C. PAPÉ.
The volume contains the first and second parts of the famous 'progress'.

Anthony Hope's THE PRISONER OF ZENDA. Illustrated by MICHAEL GODFREY.
The great Ruritanian romance.

Daniel Defoe's ROBINSON CRUSOE. Illustrated by J. AYTON-SYMINGTON.
An illustrated version which matches Defoe's great adventure story.

Anthony Hope's RUPERT OF HENTZAU. Illustrated by MICHAEL GODFREY.
The enthralling sequel to *The Prisoner of Zenda*.

H. W. Longfellow's SONG OF HIAWATHA. Illustrated by KIDDELL-MONROE.
The romantic beauty of the legends imaginatively depicted.

TEN TALES OF DETECTION. Edited by ROGER LANCELYN GREEN.
Conan Doyle's Sherlock Holmes and other famous detectives of fiction.
Illustrated by IAN RIBBONS.

John Buchan's THE THIRTY-NINE STEPS. Illustrated by EDWARD ARDIZZONE.
One of the most exciting of Secret Service novels.

Mark Twain's TOM SAWYER
 HUCKLEBERRY FINN
These two Twain classics are superbly illustrated by C. WALTER HODGES.

Ernest Thompson Seton's THE TRAIL OF THE SANDHILL STAG and Other
Lives of the Hunted. Illustrated with drawings by the author and coloured
frontispiece by RITA PARSONS.

Jules Verne's TWENTY THOUSAND LEAGUES UNDER THE SEA. Illustrated
by WILLIAM MCLAREN.
Adventures of the submarine *Nautilus*.

Robert Louis Stevenson's TREASURE ISLAND. Illustrated by S. VAN ABBÉ.
Probably no other illustrator of this famous tale has portrayed so vividly the
characters in a book that lives so long in a boy's imagination.

Frank L. Baum's THE WONDERFUL WIZARD OF OZ. Illustrated by B. S. BIRO.

Further volumes in preparation